Literacy Matters

D1344449

Second Edition

Literacy Matters

Strategies Every Teacher Can Use

Robin Fogarty

Second Edition

CORWIN PRESS
A SAGE Publications Company
Thousand Oaks, CA 91320

For information:

Corwin Press
A Sage Publications Company
2455 Teller Road
Thousand Oaks, California 91320
www.corwinpress.com

Sage Publications Ltd.
1 Oliver's Yard
55 City Road
London EC1Y 1SP
United Kingdom

Sage Publications India Pvt. Ltd.
B-42, Panchsheel Enclave
Post Box 4109
New Delhi 110 017 India

Printed in the United States of America.

Library of Congress Cataloging-in-Publication Data

Fogarty, Robin.
Literacy matters: Strategies every teacher can use / Robin Fogarty.—2nd ed.
    p. cm.
Includes bibliographical references and index.
ISBN 1-4129-3890-2 or 978-1-412938-90-7 (cloth)
ISBN 1-4129-3891-0 or 978-1-412928-91-4 (pbk.)
  1. Language arts. 2. Reading. I. Title.

LB1576.F62 2007
372.6—dc22
                                    2006026350

This book is printed on acid-free paper.

06   07   08   09   10   11   9 8 7 6 5 4 3 2 1

Acquisitions Editor:	Jean Ward
Editorial Assistant:	Jordon Barbakow
Production Editor:	Diane S. Foster
Copy Editor:	Karen E. Taylor
Typesetter:	C&M Digitals (P) Ltd.
Proofreader:	Dorothy Hoffman
Indexer:	Molly Hall
Cover Designer:	Anthony Paular
Graphic Designer:	Audrey Snodgrass

Contents

Acknowledgments

I want to acknowledge three people who have had significant impact on my thinking about the meaning of reading and about "literacy matters" in general: Dr. Christine Rauscher, Dr. Nelda Hobbs and Cynthia Nesselroade. They helped me immensely with their fellowship as caring educators.

I remember, as though it were yesterday, the question Dr. Rauscher asked me years ago in Palatine, Illinois, School District #15, where she serves as Assistant Superintendent for Curriculum and Instruction. She said, simply, "What is reading?" In the simplicity of this question lies its complexity. What is reading? My answer: Reading is a window to the world. Of course, there are lots of other more technical answers, but that's the answer that makes the act of reading so compelling and an urgent educational concern.

When I lamented to my friend, Dr. Hobbs, that I couldn't find a citation for the SQ3R strategy, she casually said, "It's Robinson." How did she know that off the top of her head? She knew that because she knows reading. After thirty plus years with the Chicago Public Schools, she knows this: If kids can't read, they can't do anything else. And she dedicates her work, in retirement, to helping teachers help kids to read.

And finally, last, but not least, I want to thank Cynthia for her comradeship during my year of literacy coaching in her native state of West Virginia. Her expertise and our conversations served me well. I will be forever grateful.

Thanks to these three educators for their knowledge, expertise, and uncommon commitment to "literacy matters."

Robin Fogarty
Chicago, IL

Corwin Press gratefully acknowledges the contributions of the following individuals:

David B. Cohen, MA Ed., NBCT
English / Reading Teacher
Palo Alto High School
Palo Alto, CA

David Barringer
English Teacher/Forensics Coach
Oregon City High School
Oregon City, Oregon

Brigitte Ness
Literacy Coach
Bennett Elementary School
Bennett, Colorado

Gayla LeMay
8th Grade Middle School Teacher
Radloff Middle School
Duluth, Georgia

Cristen L. Krugh
English Teacher
Edgewater High School
Orlando, Florida

About the Author

Robin Fogarty, PhD, is President of Robin Fogarty and Associates, Ltd., a Chicago-based, minority-owned educational publishing/consulting company. Her doctorate is in curriculum and human resource development from Loyola University of Chicago. A leading proponent of the thoughtful classroom, she has trained educators throughout the world in curriculum, instruction, and assessment strategies. She has taught at all levels, from kindergarten to college, served as an administrator, and consulted with state departments and ministries of education in the United States, Puerto Rico, Russia, Canada, Australia, New Zealand, Germany, Great Britain, Singapore, Korea, and the Netherlands. She has published articles in *Educational Leadership, Phi Delta Kappan,* and the *Journal of Staff Development.* She is the author of numerous publications, including *Brain-Compatible Classrooms; Ten Things New Teachers Need; Literacy Matters; How to Integrate the Curricula; The Adult Learner; A Look at Transfer; Close the Achievement Gap; Twelve Brain Principles; Nine Best Practices;* and most recently, with Brian Pete, *From Staff Room to Classroom: Planning and Coaching Professional Learning.*

To the science teacher,
the math teacher,
the social studies teacher,
the art, music, P.E., and special needs teacher.
While not the reading teacher,
Each is a teacher of literacy.

—Robin Fogarty

Introduction

1

- 90 million Americans lack basic literacy skills;
- American businesses lose $60 million each year due to lack of employees' basic reading skills.

Ms. Juanita Ramirez: I think we've got our priorities confused. If we can't teach our children to read, when that is what they come to school to learn—you know, you've heard the little ones . . . "What are you going to learn in school? I'm going to learn to read!"—what's going on, why can't we reach them?

Mr. Lou McGuire: I agree. A nation as wealthy as ours has no business neglecting the education of our children. Why can't we teach our kids to read? If literacy truly is a national priority, all children would read, and they would want to read. They'd know they owned the key to lifelong literacy and learning.

Ms. Juanita Ramirez: Now, you've got me thinking. It's the $64,000 question. How did I learn how to read? I think I was just read to by my parents, and I learned the books by heart. I would say all of the words right along with my Dad. Do you have a first memory of learning to read?

Mr. Lou McGuire: I remember going to the library every Saturday. Mrs. Gerad, our librarian, would read a special story, and then we would find a book to take home.

Ms. Juanita Ramirez: You know, I have an idea. What if we ask our students how they learned to read. And, then, we can have them ask their parents the same question. This could be a way to begin to put a huge emphasis on reading.

Mr. Lou McGuire: I really like your idea. We can start with the $64,000 question about learning how to read, and then we can pursue this line of student-parent dialogue with other questions:

What do you like to read?

What do you read the most?

Do you like to read?

Or, do you like writing, better?

Ms. Juanita Ramirez: Wow! I think we are on to something. These are exactly the kinds of conversations I want my students to be having this year as we focus on literacy skills of all kinds.

Mr. Lou McGuire: Well, here they come. Time to greet the little darlings!

ABOUT THE BOOK

Based on the premise that, while not all teachers are reading teachers, all are teachers of literacy, *Literacy Matters* addresses teachers working with students across all content areas and across all grade levels. The teaching and learning strategies support and advance literacy, within the context of the various subject areas. Using these stand-alone strategies with social studies content, or with the concepts of science, math, or literature, teachers explicitly incorporate the elements for reading, writing, speaking, and listening into their content-specific lessons.

The organization of the book is not meant to move sequentially from one chapter to the next, although it can be read and reviewed that way. Because each of the strategies work independently of the others, readers may peruse the table of contents or skim and scan the various sections of the book and dip in and out of the areas that seem most pertinent to their needs. Some may want to dive into the section on guided reading immediately, even though it appears at the end of the book, while others may prefer to start with the first strategy in the book, the learning to learn strategies that foster metacognitive reflection. As it is a small handbook of ideas, the system of offering optional approaches works quite easily, regardless of how one maneuvers through the various sections.

THE ACRONYM: LITERACY MATTERS

For those not trained in reading instruction, *Literacy Matters* offers over 45 strategies that encourage students in the development of their literacy skills. Each letter of *Literacy Matters* represents a set of instructional activities that unpack a literacy skill. The various sections are arranged in the following order:

L-I-T-E-R-A-C-Y M-A-T-T-E-R-S

Learn to learn with metacognitive reflections

Interact with seven strategies to comprehend

Tap into prior knowledge to support schema theory

Extend reading to encourage flexible reading

Research the principles of the brain and learning

Analyze words to foster fluency

Collaborate with cooperative learning groups to engage learners

You-are-a-reader attitude matters

Mediate with early intervention strategies

Appeal to parents/guardians and get them involved

Teach vocabulary by building background knowledge

Tune in to technology to impact literacy

Enter literacy with a multiple intelligences approach

Read aloud, read along, read appropriately to foster flexible readers

Strategize with guided reading activities

Literacy Matters defines each of these sets of strategies and offers best practices teachers can use to help improve student literacy while using their subject matter materials. *Literacy Matters* is a practical guide for enhancing literacy skills at any grade level and in any content area.
Enjoy!

—Robin Fogarty
Chicago, IL

Learn to Learn With Metacognitive Reflections

Learning how to learn is just as important as what one is learning—going beyond the cognitive and into the realm of the metacognitive. Metacognition is about planning, monitoring, and evaluating one's own thinking and learning. To illustrate the concept of metacognition, think about a student working a typical mathematics problem. The cognitive part of the lesson is the answer to the problem. The metacognitive part (Flavell, 1979) is the student's awareness of the strategy he or she used to solve the problem and to arrive at the answer.

When the teacher focuses the lesson on the strategy as well as the answer, the student thinks about how he or she solves problems, and those strategies become part of the student's repertoire for future problems in mathematics as well as in other disciplines. By reflecting on the lesson, the student generalizes the learning and can apply it in diverse and novel situations.

> Metacognition is about planning, monitoring, and evaluating.

Learning to learn, or metacognition, is about becoming aware of one's strengths and weaknesses as a learner. It is about acting on that awareness to change the way one does things. Once the learner is aware, that learner gains control over future learning situations. Teachers must explicitly weave metacognitive strategies into the fabric of the teaching-learning process. Metacognition is about planning, monitoring, and evaluating. It is easily integrated into the thinking processes before, during, and after the lesson.

USE MEDIATED JOURNALS BEFORE THE LESSON

It is often appropriate to define terms prior to the lesson; therefore, an examination of the term literacy serves as a way to illustrate using metacognition before the lesson. Literacy is a robust concept that can be somewhat ambiguous. What is the definition of literacy as it applies to reading? To help develop a personal definition of literacy, try the following reflective strategy with students, a strategy using mediated journal writing.

A mediated journal entry is an entry with prompts by the teacher that cue the student to respond. The prompts get the student thinking by "priming the pump." Using the concept of the mediated journal entry, have students respond to the following prompts to describe a literate person:

1. Name someone you believe is literate (personal acquaintance, celebrity, historical figure, or fictional character).

2. List two traits of the literate person you selected.

3. Describe someone who is not a literate person.

4. Tell how the two are different.

5. Write a summary sentence.

6. Title your piece: A Literate Person.

Illiterate (can't read) or Alliterate (does not read)

After completing the journal entry, think about the benefits of being a literate person and the repercussions of being illiterate (can't read) or alliterate (does not read). Some issues you might include are self-esteem, school and grades, open doors, or the gatekeeper concept of "closed gateways" to higher education and other opportunities.

USE LITERACY RANKING DURING THE LESSON

During the lesson, teachers can further examine the elements of literacy by having students rank the four elements of literacy according to strengths: reading, writing, speaking, and listening. Students can then justify their rankings of literacy elements with further reflection (see Figure 1).

Literacy Ranking

Rank the elements of literacy according to your strengths:

_____ Reading

_____ Writing

_____ Speaking

_____ Listening

Think about how you might pursue your weaker areas and why you might want to pursue them.

Figure 1

Mr. Parnes's questions can spark thinking and metacognition during the act of reading. Ask students to use Mr. Parnes's questions as they read: "Pause at key points and ask yourself, 'How does this connect to something I already know? How might I use this in the future?'" As students learn to mentally gauge the possibilities of these two reflective questions, they begin to interact with the reading in the most meaningful ways.

Best Practice

RETURN TO MEDIATED JOURNALS AFTER THE LESSON

Again, a proven tool for explicit attention to reflective learning following the learning is the mediated journal, which guides the student entry with lead-ins (Fogarty, 1994). Lead-ins do just that. They lead the student to write a reflection. A lead-in leads students to think in critical and creative ways. Notice how the various lead-ins dictate a certain kind of thinking on the part of the student:

I wonder . . .

A conclusion I have drawn is . . .

Comparing the two . . .

What if . . . ?

A problem I'm having is . . .

The easiest part was . . .

My worry is . . .

How might I . . . ?

As students respond to the lead-ins, they begin to solidify their thinking about the learning, and they begin to develop a keen awareness about how they learn. This kind of self-feedback is critical to the concepts of lifelong literacy and learning.

Reading, writing, speaking, and listening are inextricably linked in the journey toward becoming a literate person.

Reading, writing, speaking, and listening are inextricably linked in the journey toward becoming a literate person. Use the mediated journal as a literacy tool to prompt thinking prior to the lesson and again following the lesson as a review tool to deepen comprehension. Have students label various sections of the journal. Use labels such as the following:

- Vocabulary
- Summaries

- Characters to Remember
- Great Beginnings
- Literary Illuminations
- Write Your Own Endings
- Kinds of Stories I Like

Discuss with students how these labels are not only helpful signals about the important information to capture when reading but also helpful ways to categorize thoughts following the reading to capture the key points. Compare the mediated journal to typical text organizers such as headings, boldface type, and italics. Talk about how the text organizers and mediated entries act as signals to the reader or learner to pay closer attention.

Interact With Seven Strategies to Comprehend (Phantom Skill)

~~~
❦
~~~

Comprehension is an interesting concept. It is often referred to as a skill, and, in fact, it is considered the key skill in reading. Yet, it is also called the "phantom skill." While teachers talk about comprehension and reference it frequently, as one examines the intricacies of reading instruction, one finds that the skill of comprehension is not explicitly taught.

To improve comprehension, teachers can teach active reading strategies. An active reader is an interactive reader. Interactive readers use seven key interactions as they read (Keene & Zimmerman, 1997). The seven strategies are as follows:

Schema theory

Asking questions

Finding themes

Visualizing

Making inferences

Summarizing

Using fix up strategies.

Each of the seven is briefly discussed in the following section.

SCHEMA THEORY

Interactive readers use their schema theory to activate prior knowledge and to find connections between what they are reading and what they already know. While this is more thoroughly discussed in the section called "Tap Into Prior Knowledge," it makes sense to mention it here also, as it is one of the magic seven strategies that increase comprehension. Schema theory refers to the knowledge that the learner brings to the learning—to what the learner knows that might connect to the new, incoming information.

ASK QUESTIONS

Interactive readers ask questions of themselves, the author, and the entire context of what they are reading.

> **Interactive readers ask questions of themselves, the author, and the entire context of what they are reading.**

Asking questions of *themselves* might include the following musings: Have I ever done anything like this myself? Do I know anyone like this? Is this connected to my life in any way?

Asking questions of the *author* might encompass probing the assumptions and biases of the author as the reader reads between the lines.

Asking questions about the entire *context* might sound like this: Mood? Tone? Setting? Facts? Descriptions? What is this all about? What is going on here? What is going to happen next? What does this really mean?

To encourage all readers to model what good readers do, teachers can use the read-think scenario. The memory cue is read-think, read-think, read-think. The questioning cue is "What am I thinking? Why am I thinking that?" These are the types of questions that foster an internal dialogue in the mind of the reader. Not only do readers anticipate what is to come by asking questions, but they also justify their thoughts by linking them to facts in the text. Initially, teachers need to make these cues explicit and somewhat exaggerated for emphasis, but eventually the read-think scenario becomes quite fluid. In fact, it becomes embedded in the process of the effective reader.

IMPORTANT THEMES

> **Readers know how to identify key ideas and how to ignore the less important ones.**

Interactive readers find important themes that help them to comprehend the information. They know what is important and what is not. They can skim and scan to comprehend quickly. These readers know how to identify key ideas and how to ignore the less important ones. This skill becomes more urgent as the reading becomes more sophisticated and complex.

MAKE INFERENCES

The read-think strategy fosters inquiry because the reader is forever trying to make inferences and draw conclusions from the text. There are three levels of processing that provide the needed practice for reading between the lines or making good inferences as one reads. These include concrete, representational, and abstract activities. Figure 2 shows how teachers can use these three levels of activities effectively to develop the concept of making inferences and understanding the implied meaning.

To read between the lines, readers go beyond the given information and make inferences about what is happening (Anderson, Hiebert, Scott, & Wilkinson, 1985). For example, when an author writes "The woman returned to the porch, drenched from head to foot," readers can infer that, if the woman is drenched, she is very wet. Then, readers think about how she became drenched and conclude that it is probably raining. If the woman is drenched, it must be raining quite hard. Readers have to think and picture what the words are saying to understand what is happening. Readers have to question, wonder, and inquire as they read.

Readers have to question, wonder, and inquire as they read.

VISUALIZE

"If the words remain words and sit quietly on the page; if they remain nouns, and verbs and adjectives, then we are truly blind. But, if words seem to disappear and our innermost self begins to laugh and cry, to sing and dance, and finally to fly . . . if we are transformed in all that we are, to a brand new world, then . . . and only then . . . can we READ" (Wayman, 1980, p. 1).

The skill of visualization is a skill of literacy, of learning, and of life.

The skill of visualization is a skill of literacy, of learning, and of life. To be able to visualize the story in one's mind from the words on the page is what Wayman describes so beautifully. Visualization is critical to the reading process, but it is critical to learning and to life as well. The skill of visualization is the skill of goal setting—seeing oneself in a future time and place. It is the skill of achieving excellence—seeing one's self cross the finish line in record time. It is the skill of wellness—seeing oneself healthy and strong.

Visualization is critical to the reading process, but it is critical to learning and to life as well.

Making Inferences

Concrete Experience: Reading body language and facial expressions or reading the audience.

Have students role-play various body stances and/or facial expressions: mad, happy, friendly, scared, cold, shy, hot, sad, miserable, joyful . . .

Representational Experience: Reading the implied humor in comics, cartoons, and political cartoons

Use three comic strip boxes with a picture in the middle box only. Then have students infer what happened in the first picture and predict what might happen in the last picture.

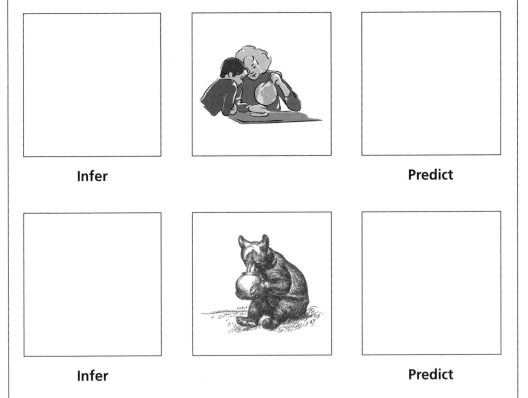

| Infer | | Predict |

Abstract Experience: Reading between the lines (going beyond the given information) to draw conclusions (understand the implied meaning of written text).

Have students read a passage and find the implied mood or setting. Use a one-page story or excerpt for them to extrapolate the setting.

Figure 2

Use visualization strategies to train students to become better at visualizing. Begin by asking students to think back and recreate images of their bedrooms to determine if the door opens out into the hallway or into the bedroom. Have them recall the refrigerator in their kitchens. Tell them to open the refrigerator door and, using the mind's eye, find the ketchup bottle. Ask them whether it is full or almost empty. Is it clean or messy?

Then, ask them to think about the times they visualized a new toy or game they wanted or the times when they savored the flavor of a favorite dish Mom cooked. Ask students how often they use the visualization skill.

Next, follow up the memory activity by showing some pictures of optical illusions. Have students sense the shift in perception as they move from one image to the other and try to visualize the two very different pictures. Show them a series of numbers. Hide the numbers, and ask them to recall the series by visualizing the sequence.

Finally, connect visualization to reading. Read aloud a scene from a story, and ask students to visualize the scene as they recreate the image on paper. Discuss how active readers constantly make pictures in their minds as they read, that is, visualize what they see using the mind's eye. Suggest that students use this strategy over and over as visualization helps them make meaning of the text.

SUMMARIZE

Best Practice

Being able to summarize aids as well as verifies comprehension. Readers can summarize when they are able to succinctly tell about the main idea, give a synopsis, or give the "gist" of the text they have just read. They know that a summary is very different from a sequential retelling of the piece. They understand that a summary is not a "bed to bed story" that meanders from the beginning of the event to the end. For example, they do not say, " I got up, and I did this; then I did this, and I did this, and then I went to bed." Rather, they give a brief synopsis of the highlights.

> **They understand that a summary is not a "bed to bed story" that meanders from the beginning of the event to the end.**

FIX UP STRATEGIES

Best Practice

Interactive readers use fix up strategies to help them stay connected to the text. They are aware when they have lost contact with the text and have recovery strategies to get back on track. These include rereading; looking for key words; rereading first and last sentences; finding italicized words or bold face words; trying to pick up a thought; noticing a picture, chart, or figure on the same page; and various and sundry other recovery strategies.

Tap Into Prior Knowledge to Support Schema Theory

———————— ⚜ ————————

S chema theory (Pearson, 1986), as mentioned earlier, is about comprehending what one reads. Based on the constructivist view of learning, schema theory states that the learner possesses an individually held, personal schema of things in his or her mind. This schema is constructed through the background knowledge and life experiences of the learner. Schema theory suggests that each reader brings a different schema to the reading, based on his or her background knowledge and life experiences. To read with comprehension, readers must somehow connect the incoming information with the existing scheme in their minds. They must make sense of the input based on what they already know.

> Schema theory suggests that each reader brings a different schema to the reading, based on his or her background knowledge and life experiences.

Readers tap into prior knowledge in three distinct ways. They find connections between text and self, text and other text, and text and the world as they know it. These connections allow the reader to literally connect the new information to the old information in their heads. It is how synapses are developed in the human brain and how the brain actually learns. As the brain grows dendrites, it creates synapses between brain cells. The result is what is known as learning.

Text-to-self connections involve the learner making a relevant connection of the incoming input to personal experiences. For example, a

Text-to-self connections involve the learner making a relevant connection of the incoming input to personal experiences.

reader might read something about Native American arts and culture and connect it immediately to the personal experience of a trip to Santa Fe, New Mexico, and the various art forms evidenced there in the museums.

Text-to-text connections encompass opportunities for the reader to make critical linkages from the text she or he is reading to another text read earlier or at another time. This is illustrated by the reader who connects narratives with informational texts: a story about the sea, such as "The Old Man and the Sea," with an encyclopedia entry on marlins of the sea.

Text to world connections are meaningful connections that the reader makes between the reading and world events and occurrences. For instance, as students are learning about natural disasters, they may connect the information in the textbook to real world earthquakes, mudslides, and aftershocks that they see on the television newscast.

If schema theory is true, it is critical to stir up that prior knowledge before learners read to help each reader connect the new to the old. It may be more important for teachers to spend time before the reading to create a mindset for what is going to be read than to spend the time after the reading to check on what students comprehended.

Tapping into prior knowledge seems to be the pre-reading strategy that leads to deep understanding. Knowing that learning is a function of experience, teachers can enable pre-reading experiences that provide an essential link to reading comprehension.

One way teachers can help students understand is to ask students to *agree or disagree* with statements about the reading prior to the reading and then again after the reading to compare their ideas. The second way is to ask students to make predictions using the *KWL strategy* (Ogle, 1989) to determine what they know, what they want to know, and what they have learned through the KWL strategy.

These kinds of pre-learning strategies promote deep understanding of the reading by putting the emphasis on prior knowledge. The search for meaning is based on the individual scheme of each learner. Each reader's meaning-seeking mechanism—called the brain—fosters connection making and actually creates the neural pathways in the mind of the learner. These pathways are the pathways that enhance memory and learning. In fact, they are necessary for the patterning to occur that chunks the learning for short- and long-term memory (Sylwester, 1995).

Schema theory makes a case for pre-learning strategies that tap into prior knowledge.

Schema theory makes a case for pre-learning strategies that tap into prior knowledge. The triangle and the inverted triangle illustrate the traditional and the constructivist way of approaching reading (see Figure 3). Teachers can share these illustrations with students as

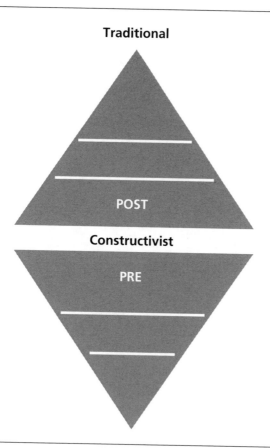

Figure 3

they discuss why they spend time stirring up ideas prior to reading, rather than merely checking up after the reading.

Instead of spending the majority of the time on recall of ideas to check for comprehension after the reading, teachers need to give more time and attention to bringing up prior knowledge before and during the reading. In this way, readers are ready, with the proper mindset, to accept the incoming input. The connection making is facilitated as the reader links prior knowledge to new information.

USE AN AGREE/DISAGREE CHART

Another strategy for activating prior knowledge is through the agree/disagree chart. To use this evaluation tool, prepare a listing of statements about the topic for readers to agree or disagree with prior to the reading (see Figure 4 as a sample). Then revisit the statements following the reading to validate answers or allow changes, revisions, or additions to initial thinking about the statements.

Agree/Disagree		
	BEFORE **Agree Disagree**	**AFTER** **Agree Disagree**
1. Alcohol kills brain cells.		
2. A glass of beer and wine have equal amounts of alcohol.		
3. Marijuana is legal.		
4. Cocaine addiction is chronic, progressive, and fatal.		
5. Prescription drugs are safe.		

Figure 4

THE KWL CHART

The KWL chart (Ogle, 1989) is another prior knowledge strategy that is powerful to use in K–12 classrooms. Teachers can use a KWL chart (see Figure 5) with students as they discuss the topic or idea they are about to study or read about.

Before reading, have students complete (individually or as a class) the "What we **K**now" and "What we **W**ant to know" columns. Following the reading, ask students to complete the "What we **L**earned" column. The KWL chart is an efficient way for teachers, as well as students, to find out what students know before the lesson begins.

PEOPLE SEARCH

A third strategy is to use the "people search" to stir up prior knowledge. In this strategy, the teacher writes several statements to complete the phrase "find someone who . . ." and asks the learners to search for individuals matching these descriptive statements. As participants move about, talking to various people, they uncover information about each of the statements. The following people search is an example of how to stir up prior knowledge about the math concept of probability.

Math People Search: Probability

Find someone who . . .

1. Makes a bet and will explain how he or she determined what to bet on.

2. Knows how the stats on a racehorse help determine the odds for the race.

3. Explains the differences among the following three futuristic words:
   Possible   Probable   Preferable

4. Offers an opinion on the stock market and tells why.

5. Analyzes the "flip of a coin" as a fair or unfair practice for deciding.

6. Tells how graphs and charts depict information that can be used to determine probabilities.

7. Knows how to explain this statement: "The odds are good, but the goods are odd."

8. Beat the odds in a real world situation and will tell how.

KWL Chart		
What we *Know*	What we *Want* to know	What we *Learned*

Figure 5

Extend Reading to Encourage Flexible Reading

Good readers read extensively. They read in a variety of settings: silently and mentally to themselves, orally to and with others, and in school with guided reading in groups using particular cueing strategies. Good readers read fiction and nonfiction. They read fiction in many ways through different kinds of literature (called genres) that might include the following: poetry, novels, short stories, folktales, fairytales, tall tales, children's stories, adventure stories, mysteries, science fiction, fantasy, and three-act plays.

> **Good readers read fiction and nonfiction.**

Good readers read all kinds of nonfiction as well. They read biographies and autobiographies, memoirs, articles, essays, critiques and reviews, newspaper editorials and features, and political commentary. They read pamphlets, instruction manuals, brochures, newsletters, memos, and e-mails. Good readers read friendly letters, business letters, greeting cards, posters, and billboards. In short, good readers read. They read everything, everywhere, all the time. In fact, evidence suggests that the gap, sometimes called the Matthews Effect (Stanovich, 1986), between good readers and poor readers widens over time as good readers continue to read all the time, and poor readers continue not to read over much time. Poor readers seem never to catch up.

When teachers encourage students to read extensively in various settings and to sample different genres, readers become familiar, fluent,

When teachers encourage students to read extensively in various settings and to sample different genres, readers become familiar, fluent, and flexible with the various types of reading material they encounter throughout life.

and flexible with the various types of reading material they encounter throughout life. Teachers can sample student reading preferences by asking students about their preferences, which is a beginning to a lively discussion comparing and contrasting genres. These types of discussions heighten the awareness of nonreaders as they begin to explore the regions of reading, and it propels students who are already voracious readers to investigate new genres.

THE HUMAN GRAPH—AN INTERACTIVE EXPERIENCE

Best Practice

Reading, or "reading reading," distinguishes reading time in the classroom that is not for specific skill development but rather for just plain old reading—reading that is just for the enjoyment of reading. This is the time to begin to develop the-kind-of-book-I-like or my-favorite-author attitudes that readers achieve by sampling a range of genres and authors. To initiate this in the classroom, teachers might use an interactive experience called the human graph to begin the conversation about what is appealing to eager readers and not so eager readers.

This is the time to begin to develop the-kind-of-book-I-like or my-favorite-author attitudes.

To try this highly motivating activity, have students respond to the human graph by going to one side of the room or the other, basing their preferences on one of the reading choices listed after Figure 6 (a human graph example).

1. Fiction or Nonfiction

2. Mysteries or Histories

3. Biographies or Autobiographies

4. Tall Tales or Folktales

5. Limericks or Haiku

6. Narrative or Procedural

As the teacher calls out each of the above choices, the students literally move to the designated side of the room. After each move to a category of choice, have students talk with others in their areas about why they made the choices they made. Sample some of their thoughts. You may use the six choices noted above (1–6) to design lesson introductions

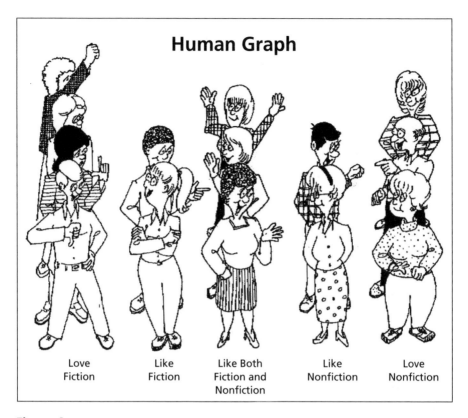

Figure 6

to each of the genres listed. This practice motivates students to think about the various genres they might want to sample.

The human graph is also useful as students read a story. Just ask them to choose one character or another, one plot line or another, or one setting or another. It is a great way to get them involved in the story once they have found a genre they like.

USE A VENN DIAGRAM
TO COMPARE AND CONTRAST

Best Practice

Reading is flexible. Introduce students to various genres, including poetry, textbooks, recipes, instructions, articles, and e-mail. Have students use a Venn diagram to compare and contrast two very different kinds of reading material (see Figure 7 as an example). Discuss the genre and the myriad elements of each that create the richness of a particular reading through the sounds of language, story and plot lines, headlines and graphics, and their relationship to literacy.

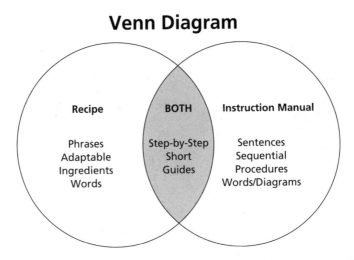

Venn Diagram

Recipe

Phrases
Adaptable
Ingredients
Words

BOTH

Step-by-Step
Short
Guides

Instruction Manual

Sentences
Sequential
Procedures
Words/Diagrams

Figure 7

Best Practice

INFORMATIONAL TEXT AND NARRATIVE TEXT

Encouraging students to become flexible readers is supported through the context of reading two very different kinds of texts: informational text and narrative text. In the real world, literate people read both kinds of text as they move through the day. One example of a typical day of reading both narrative and informational text might look something like this. The day begins with a narrative selection from a book of meditations. Then, informational text comes into play with a quick glance at the headlines in the daily newspaper. Much of the day is consumed reading informational text at the workplace as the various papers, letters, e-mails, and memos circulate through the day's work. Narrative text might be read in selecting a greeting card, reading a chapter from a novel that evening, or reading and writing personal e-mails to family and friends.

> Encouraging students to become flexible readers is supported through the context of reading two very different kinds of texts: informational text and narrative text.

Similarly, students read both informational and narrative text as their day progresses. Yet a startling fact remains. In the elementary school years, 90 percent of the reading is with narrative text, as students read stories and selections from their readers. However, in the high school years, 90 percent of the reading is with informational text, as students read in their textbooks from the various disciplines. With that fact in mind, educators have begun a pressing movement to include more informational text in the daily reading of the younger students to prepare them more fully for the comprehension of informational text as they enter the middle years and high school years.

A powerful strategy for comprehending informational text is cited in the last chapter of this book, Strategize Reading with Guided Reading Activities. There, the SQ3R strategy is fully explained and discussed. On the other hand, two strategies to foster the comprehension of narrative text also appear in the same, final chapter of the book: the Directed Reading and Thinking Activity (DRTA) and the BET strategy.

Research the Principles of the Brain and Learning

The emerging research on mind, memory, and learning supports sound pedagogy and also provides new insights about how the brain works. Naturally, this information impacts the literacy community. For example, the concept of constructivism, which holds that the learner constructs meaning in the mind by connecting new information to prior knowledge, is supported by the fact that dendrites, root-like characters that extend from the brain cell to receive messages (Sylwester, 1995), continue to grow and interconnect throughout one's lifetime. Further research suggests that dendritic growth can be stimulated by rich environments (Diamond & Hopson, 1998). This logically includes print-rich environments that foster literacy.

The mind typically holds seven bits of information, plus or minus two. In addition, the concept that memory is stored throughout the brain and can be triggered by any number of sensory stimuli supports the idea of stimulating prior knowledge before reading, as already discussed. The fact that the mind typically holds seven bits of information, plus or minus two, supports a method called chunking of information for ease of memory. Chunking means that certain data are remembered as one collective set, or chunk, for easier recall. It facilitates the learning and remembering of discrete bits of information.

Think of the mind as a mind map.

Another piece of research links emotion to memory and points once again to the critical role past experiences play in the teaching-learning process. To visualize how dendrites develop into an eco-jungle system in the brain, think of the mind as a mind map. Think of themes, such as the ones used in curriculum development, that provide a means to explicit connection making, and think of chunking as a way to facilitate short-term memory by connecting information as one is learning it. In the United States, HOMES is a meaningful chunk that helps one remember the names of the five Great Lakes:

Huron

Ontario

Michigan

Erie

Superior

While these examples just touch the tip of the research iceberg on how the brain learns, they serve to illustrate the powerful linkage between theory and practice.

SENSORY MEMORY TO STORAGE (OR LONG-TERM MEMORY)

Emerging research on the brain and learning sheds light on important aspects of the mind, memory, and learning. Using concepts from the research on the brain and learning, think about the following statement and agree or disagree with it:

The brain is more like a sieve than it is like a sponge.

If one agrees with the statement, then one can begin to understand the saying "Memory, the thing I forget with." While it is a bit of a joke, there is the seed of reality in the paradoxical statement. The brain is designed to pay attention to important information and to let go of extraneous information that it does not seem to need. Therefore it does, indeed, act more like a sieve by sifting for the big chunks of information and sifting out the inconsequential.

To understand more fully how the memory and learning system works in the human brain, think about another metaphor, which uses the concept of the computer screen. The memory follows this metaphorical scenario:

It's on my screen (sensory memory).

It's on my desktop (short-term memory).

It's on my menu (working memory).

It's on my hard drive (storage and long-term memory).

It's on My Screen (Sensory Memory)

It's on the screen means that some sensory input gets one's attention, which is the first stage of memory. Because of something's novelty, relevance, or meaning, the mind attends to the input. The brain notices the sensory input. For example, a teacher attends a conference and hears that the educational concern is not about technology but rather about the impact of technology. This idea catches the teacher's attention because the teacher is working with computers at school.

> Because of something's novelty, relevance, or meaning, the mind attends to the input.

It's on My Desktop (Short-Term Memory)

When a person makes sense of the input by connecting it to something he or she already knows, the information is in short-term memory—it is on the computer's desktop. The teacher in the above example thinks about how technology impacts literacy, and now the information goes into short-term memory. Or, because it is causing dissonance and not connecting properly to something he or she already knows, the teacher is even more aware of the input, and it still goes into short-term memory.

It's on My Menu (Working Memory)

Next, a person actually uses the new information in some way, and it goes on the menu, which represents the working memory. The teacher takes the idea to his or her team and suggests that the team work on the impact of technology and how it changes the reading and writing program plans. Now it is in working memory because the teacher is actually using the information.

It's on My Hard Drive (Storage and Long-Term Memory)

Finally, as the teacher continues to massage the information about the impact of technology, the teacher notices a shift from concern about computers to concern and planning about the curricular impact of computers. The new learning is now on the teacher's "hard drive," and it pops up from long-term memory where it is stored until it is needed.

Have students follow the metaphor of the computer screen to describe a personal example of how they have remembered something, and ask them to use as many of the four stages of short- and long-term memory as they can. Share and sample some. Then, talk about how mind mapping depicts the pathways the mind takes as it connects to various ideas. Have students create a mind map (see Figure 8 as an example) to see how it works, and then relate the mind mapping experience to memory through the concept of neural connection making. Discuss the power of themes, or big ideas, as umbrellas or natural connections that bring thoughts together in the mind of the learner.

Mind Map/Dendrite Connection

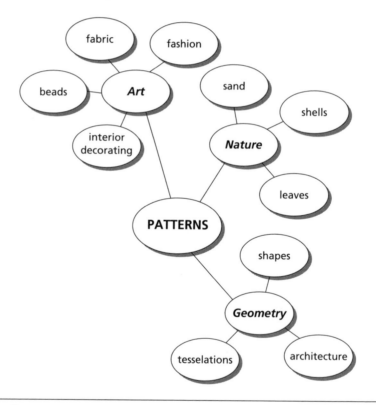

Figure 8

CHUNKING INFORMATION

Chunking, connecting ideas so that they are recalled as one coherent piece of information, is a memory technique that the mind adapts to easily. There are various chunking methods that help the mind recall bits of information. One way is through the use of mnemonics, a memory device that uses some sound or structure to recall information. HOMES, the mnemonic device for the names of the Great Lakes, was discussed earlier. The rhyme "yours is not to reason why, just invert and multiply" is another mnemonic device used as a way to remember how to divide fractions. Have students think of some mnemonics they have used to recall information, and have them share these techniques with others. Talk about how mnemonics help students remember what they read. Demonstrate how mnemonic devices help with recall and, subsequently, with comprehension for better long-term memory and application. Challenge students to create new mnemonic devices.

> Chunking, connecting ideas so that they are recalled as one coherent piece of information, is a memory technique.

Another memory device that helps chunk information is the metaphor. The three-legged stool (Waxman & Walberg, 1999) is a metaphor for educators to consider in their decision making. There are three elements that interact: the teacher, the student, and the parent. Just like a three-legged stool, all three "legs" are necessary for functionality. Invite students to think of a metaphor that works for them as they try to remember something. Discuss the power of these concrete metaphors in making abstractions more real.

One final thought about chunking concerns the 7+2 principle. The brain remembers seven bits of information, plus or minus two. Think of all the information that falls into that category: Social Security numbers, phone numbers, zip codes, seven deadly sins, seven dwarfs, seven wonders of the world. Encourage students to think of more. Then, whenever possible, explicitly chunk information into manageable pieces for easier recall. Assist students with the chunking. Over time, they become better at learning a chunk at a time and, finally, at putting things all together on their own.

THE STORY OF A BRAIN THAT READS!

Best Practice

Why is it that the same kids who learned their native language with no formal schooling have so much trouble learning to read and write? There seems to be no more urgent need in today's schools than to connect and understand how the brain learns to read, and how teachers can facilitate that process with struggling readers. In the short space below, review the agree/disagree statements and responses to get a glimpse of the research on how the brain learns to read.

> Why is it that the same kids who learned their native language with no formal schooling have so much trouble learning to read and write?

The Story of the Brain That Reads—Agree/Disagree

1. The brain is hardwired to read. **No** (Sousa, 2004, p. 29).

2. New research shows what's wrong with struggling readers . . . and what to do about it. **Not so**! (Coles, 2004, p. 346).

3. Beginning readers use Broca's area and the word analysis region of the brain to slowly analyze each word. **Yes** (Sousa, 2004, p. 51).

4. Human language is composed of neural networks. **Yes** (Coles, 2004, p. 350).

5. Only after mastering phonological awareness can beginning readers master reading skills. **Not so**! (Coles, 2004, p. 346); Yes (Shaywitz in Wingert & Kantrowitz in Sylwester, 1999, p.122).

6. Poor teaching, such as "one size fits all," is one of the many influences to produce reading problems. **Yes** (Coles, 2004, p. 346).

7. The brain learns to speak spontaneously, automatically, and naturally. **Yes** (Sousa, 2004, p. 30).

8. There are specific steps to build neural pathways deep within the brain for skilled reading. **No** (Coles, 2004, p. 346); Yes (Wingert & Kantrowitz in Sylwester, 1999, p. 123).

9. Broca's area produces language, while Wernicke's area comprehends language. **Yes** (Gutin in Sylwester, 1999, p. 107).

10. Brain research has shown that the way a child moves or follows instructions can be an indicator of how well she or he processes information. **Yes** (Wingert & Kantrowitz in Sylwester, 1999, p.125).

11. "Glitches" in the brain's wiring interfere with the ability to translate a written word into units of sound of phonemes. Yes (Wingert & Kantrowitz in Sylwester, 1999, p.122); **No** (Coles, 2004, p. 346).

12. Skilled readers rely on the word form in the occipital lobe, with marginal help from Broca's area. **Yes** (Sousa, 2004, p. 51).

13. Up to one in five kids might simply not be wired to read. **Yes** (Shaywitz in Coles, 2004, p. 346).

14. In early readers, the male brain processes language in the left hemisphere, while, the female brain processes language in both hemispheres. **Yes** (Sousa, 2004, p.12).

15. Poor readers may have disruption in the angular gyrus area, which relays word images. **Yes** (Armstrong, 2003, p. 17).

Obviously, there is much emergent research on the brain and reading. While space does not allow a fuller discussion of the brain that reads, references in the bibliography section provide resources for a more detailed look at this topic for readers who are interested.

nalyze Words to Foster Fluency

---❧---

The "reading wars" refers to an ongoing debate in which there have been two camps or two schools of thought in the educational community. Each camp of reading educators endorses an approach to teaching reading. One approach is phonics, in which word attack skills reign supreme. The other is the whole language approach, in which literature based reading takes center stage.

However, contrary to the notion of the reading wars—that battle over the ideas of a phonics approach versus a literature based approach—the reality is that both approaches work together. This "balanced" teaching philosophy is embraced by many reading teachers. While this section highlights the phonics approach, the whole language or literature based approach is discussed more fully in other sections. However, it is a combination or balance of the phonics and whole language approaches

> **This "balanced" teaching philosophy is embraced by many reading teachers.**

that is most appropriate for a comprehensive early reading program. In this section, the discussion focuses on three aspects of direct instruction for word analysis: (1) decoding, (2) contextual clues, and (3) structural analysis.

DECODING, CONTEXTUAL CLUES, AND STRUCTURAL ANALYSIS

The analysis of words (word attack skills) includes a hierarchy of sorts, beginning with sound awareness or phonemic awareness and moving to phonics and then moving from derivatives of root words, prefixes, and suffixes to contextual and structural clues. Phonemic awareness builds sound awareness; phonics builds sound-letter relationships beginning with a base of hard consonants, soft consonants, and vowels to blends, digraphs, and diphthongs, and schwa sounds.

Phonemic awareness is about building a conscious awareness of the sounds within words. The centerpiece of phonemic awareness is in music, sounds of the city, sounds of the farm, rhyming (cat, hat, sat, bat), and in sounds that are alike (sh-oe, sh-ut, sh-irt), or (f-un, f-amily, f-arm). Phonics is the skill of attaching or matching the proper sound and letter combination (b says ba, t says ta, p says pa).

Phonics, on the other hand, is about the letter-sound relationship. Once students know the letters of the alphabet, they are taught the sounds of the various letters and letter combinations. They learn the sounds of the consonants, the vowels, the blends, the digraphs, and the diphthongs. With this kind of knowledge of letter-sound relationships, students are able to "sound out" and decode words they don't know as they encounter them in their reading. Phonics is another tool in their reading skills toolbox.

Phonics is another tool in their reading skills toolbox.

The Sound Book

One practical strategy that adapts easily to the early work with decoding skills is the sound book. Teachers can use this strategy to create a sequence of sounds to teach through direct instruction. Hard consonants, blends, vowels, digraphs, and so on are taught, creating a theme for the week. Then, teachers can use that sound to develop meaningful learning experiences that put emphasis and attention on that sound.

For example, if the sound of the week is /p/, various learning experiences are structured to emphasize /p/. Youngsters might pick pumpkins, count the pumpkin seeds, and make pumpkin pie. Each day, students can complete a sound book page that stresses the focus sound through writing and composing. Teachers can send home the sound booklet at the end of the week asking students to read the booklet to anyone and everyone and collect signatures.

A major benefit of keeping a sound booklet is that, as students read the booklet over and over, they become fluent with the phonics skills.

The sound booklet works with younger and older students who need decoding emphasis because the booklet focuses on one sound, providing the needed practice.

This decoding umbrella includes the skills listed below: phonemic awareness, phonics, and derivatives.

Word Analysis: Decoding Skills

Phonemic awareness: the awareness of sounds, e.g., s=es or b=buh.

Phonics: the strategy of dissecting the letter sounds and blending them into words, e.g., D=duh o=ah g=guh.

Contextual clues: extracting the meaning of a word from the context in which it is used.

The frightened boy cowered in the corner.

"cowered"–crowded into, crouched, hid, sat

The context of the sentence sends a cue to the reader about the meaning of the word. It is a clue to unpacking the meaning of the word when the word is unknown. In the example, the meaning of the word "cowered" is hinted at by the words "frightened" and "in the corner."

Structural analysis: derivatives such as prefixes, suffixes, digraphs, and blends are used to understand meaning.

Antiestablishment . . . anti=against . . . against the establishment

Derivatives: root words with prefixes and suffixes as cues to word meaning.

Example 1: interloper—One who interferes; meddler

root word—*lopen* meaning *to run*

prefix—*inter* meaning *between*

Example 2: analysis—The separation of a whole into its parts for study

root word—*analusis* meaning *a dissolving*

suffix—*lysis* meaning *a loosening*

The mission of the educator is to help young people love to read through the skills of literacy. When readers are able to enhance their reading, writing, speaking, and listening skills in all forms of written and oral communications, their academic achievement blossoms. These are the tools of the literate person. These are the tools that make the difference between loving reading and loathing reading. The skills that create fluent and proficient readers (readers who love to read) include decoding skills.

Direct instruction in word attack skills is efficient, effective, and appropriate. Surrounding students with the awareness of the sounds around their world is the beginning. Giving them the skills to decode those sounds is the next best step. And enabling them to build their fluency and comprehension through vocabulary is the ultimate goal, for then they are reading efficiently and effectively. Reading becomes a fun activity, not a futile one.

Direct instruction in word attack skills is efficient, effective, and appropriate.

Collaborate With Cooperative Learning Groups to Engage Learners

—❦—

C ooperative learning is rated by Joyce (1999a) as the number one strategy to increase student achievement and to enhance self-esteem.

"How do I know what I think until I see what I say," is a paradoxical statement that somehow explains the thinking power of group work. As learners express their thoughts to their team partners, the thinking becomes visible to their peers and to the learners themselves.

"How do I know what I think until I see what I say?"

The strategy called literature circles (Bjorklund, Handler, Mitten, & Stockwell, 1998) taps into powerful learning experiences. Students work in small groups with a selected novel or story. They take on various roles and responsibilities as they read and discuss sections of the book. By putting thoughts from their reading into their own words, learners process the written language in terms that make sense to them. They use their speaking vocabulary to interpret the written language, and, in the process, learners clarify and crystallize their own thinking.

ESTABLISH ROLES AND RESPONSIBILITIES

Establishing the roles and responsibilities of the group members encourages all members to participate (Johnson, Johnson, Holubec, & Roy, 1984;

Best Practice

Slavin, 1983). One student leads the discussion with predetermined questions. Another shares a favorite passage, while still another might quiz members on selected vocabulary. This team effort builds a sense of trust and safety and a sense of belonging, while at the same time, building a strong understanding of what critical reading is all about. It makes reading active, interactive, and engaging for all members. In fact, as stated earlier, cooperative learning is rated by Joyce (1999a) as the number one strategy to increase student achievement and to enhance self-esteem. In over 600 studies cited by the Johnsons and others (1984), the evidence is clearly positive and convincing.

Cooperative learning makes it easier for students to ask for help in a small, safe setting. It also makes it easier for students to question, share, and critique. When teachers structure cooperative learning groups as part of the overall reading program, they also open the door to a multiple intelligences approach to literacy, which is inherent in cooperative learning. Using interpersonal intelligence as one approach, Gardner's (1983) theory suggests seven other entry points to learning: verbal/linguistic (of course), visual/spatial, logical/mathematical, musical/rhythmic, bodily/kinesthetic, intrapersonal, and the naturalist.

Working in teams, learners are able to draw their perception of a particular reading (visual), sequence the events (logical), find the rhythm of the language (musical), dramatize the reading (bodily), keep a reading response journal (intrapersonal), and discern the environmental settings of the readings (naturalist). Imagine the richness of the reading experience in these literature circles. It seems impossible not to be drawn into the web of intrigue as the plot of a story unfolds and as the members of a cooperative learning group enhance that unfolding.

Best
Practice

LITERATURE CIRCLES

Cooperative learning strategies that incorporate roles and responsibilities and involve choice within a given structure are highly effective for literacy instruction. Literature circles, based on such strategies, are one way to assist struggling readers.

Students must read at their developmental level for deep understanding and reading successes.

Similar to book clubs, literature circles (Bjorklund et al., 1998) usually consist of five or six students. If you are trying this practice with your class, note that one motivational strategy is to use standard books such as novels rather than picture books. Students often want to read more sophisticated material but need support. While students must read at their developmental level for deep understanding and reading successes, the literature circle gives students the help they need to tackle more advanced books.

To use literature circles, follow these simple steps:

1. Select themes such as friendship, trust, courage, or fear. Gather four to five books on the theme, and let students select a book and form small groups (literature circles) accordingly.

2. Some roles that teachers might assign are

   Discussion Leader: creates Socratic questions for discussion

   Wordsmith: defines significant vocabulary

   Literary Luminary: illuminates the literary sections by reading aloud

   Character Actor: role-plays characters, actions, motives, etc.

   Illustrator: captures key images from the reading

   Surveyor: graphs the plot line of the story

Naturally, the roles played in literature circles should be age appropriate and suited to students' abilities. For example, very young children might work in threes and have a storyteller, a questioner, and an artist to draw the story as it unfolds.

3. Plot the reading assignments for each book and have students meet to discuss, share, and read aloud, using the assigned roles to keep the group moving along.

4. Use a culminating day for groups to share their books with other groups, as students may want to read the other books on their own.

COOPERATIVE TEAR SHARE

Best Practice

A surefire cooperative strategy to try with younger and older readers is the cooperative tear share. It is a compelling strategy in which students are active, interactive, engaged, and invested. In this cooperative strategy, there are four students per group. They fold a blank piece of paper into four corner sections and number them 1, 2, 3, 4. In turn, the students count off: 1, 2, 3, 4. Now, all four are instructed to read the designated piece that is assigned, and all four are instructed to respond, in the appropriately numbered corner of their papers, to each of the four questions posed; student number 1 responds to questions 1–4 and so on. At this point the teacher may model an oral summary, cautioning the students not to give a running report on each of the four responses but rather to summarize the results. Each team proceeds by having its members share individual summaries and reflect on the responses and the activity itself.

Once the team has completed the reading and writing assignments, team members tear their papers into four sections, and each passes the various numbered sections to the team member of that same number. Number 1 papers go to team member number 1, number 2 papers to the number 2 student, etc. Next, the four members look over the four papers of the same number and create a summary of the responses.

The richness of this strategy is that students are actively involved in the folding, tearing, and passing of the sections. They are interactive in their sharing of the information with each other, and they are engaged in the reading and writing of their responses and in the summary of all four responses. Finally, they are invested members of the team because they know they hold one critical part of the whole.

You-Are-a-Reader Attitude Matters

———— ✧ ————

Youngsters from around the world come to school with an unmistakable mission. That mission is to learn to read. They are motivated from within. They want to read. Beyond anything else, youngsters have come to school to learn to read. Preschoolers take those magical picture books, turn the pages ever so deliberately, and mouth words to tell the story they see pictured. They gingerly select those big, fat chapter books and proudly carry them under their arms for all their friends to see. From sixteen months to sixteen years of age, youngsters can enjoy and listen attentively as someone reads aloud from a favorite storybook.

Youngsters know intrinsically that reading matters. It matters a lot. Literacy is the key that unlocks many doors in school and in life. To sustain that sense of wonder and motivation to read is every teacher's mission as well. To keep students coming back for that next book; to develop the skill and the drive for lifelong reading; to achieve fluent and flexible reading; and to help students discover that reading is informative, instructive, and enjoyable are major goals of schooling (NAEP, 1998).

> **Constant and continual feedback is a powerful tool.**

To fuel that initial thirst for reading that youngsters bring with them to school and to instill a positive you-are-a-reader attitude, teachers can use a powerful tool—constant and continual feedback (Showers, Joyce, Scalon, & Schnaubelt, 1998). This feedback sometimes is structured in the form of what Joyce (1999a) calls feedback loops. Feedback loops are data gathering tools that give students and teachers windows into the progress of the learner. For example, a feedback loop might be a graph charting the number of the books read each week or of the new vocabulary words encountered. The feedback loops might be more informal. Students might simply gather word cards or a list of unknown words encountered during one week.

Through these formal and informal feedback strategies, teachers encourage students to keep track of their reading, to keep records, and to log data that provide instant, visible, and accessible feedback about their progress. In fact, data are logged for individual students, classes, grade levels, schools, girls, and boys, so that the feedback is comprehensive and yet specific enough to allow mindful decision making. Feedback loops result in a focus that propels the readers involved to read even more.

Teachers can plot the number of books read by the class using a device such as a construction paper "caterpillar" winding around the highest boundaries of the classroom. Learners respond eagerly to such data on display. As they witness the accumulation of segments in this metaphorical representation of their work, they are inspired to read more and make the caterpillar grow. As the growing caterpillar expands and winds around the room, visual feedback is available to the students. They see every day how the reading is increasing with the class effort. These first data and feedback loops work just as they were intended (Joyce & Wolf, 1996). They inspire the competitive spirit and drive students to achieve.

Similarly, the more formalized feedback loops, such as daily, weekly, and monthly data gathering by individual students, classes within the school, and schoolwide surveys, as described by Showers and others (1998), inspire and motivate youngsters on their reading journeys. In turn, the data are available to teachers, parents, and administrators for sound decision making. When the feedback loops note that the fifth-grade boys are low in their weekly numbers, educators can intervene with swift and sure measures.

Best Practice

DATA AND FEEDBACK LOOPS

You-are-a-reader attitude means that students understand that reading matters and that they are getting good at it. It is the attitude of the "inner winner" not the "outer doubter." When teachers create data and feedback loops for good student decision making, students become invested in their own reading progress. They take ownership as they become more advanced with the graphs and charts of their reading progress. These written records empower students to do

The you-are-a-reader attitude is the attitude of the "inner winner" not the "outer doubter."

more as they see the data accumulate and their accomplishments made visible. To implement the data feedback loops or continuous, pertinent student data, have students keep charts and data logs about the types of books and authors they read. These tools are the feedback loops. As students gather data and represent data, they are able to make better decisions about their learning based on the feedback available. Help them learn to gather data to drive their work and their learning decisions. Use these ideas to set up data collection sheets for each student to use to gather data:

- Number of books per week
- Types of books (fiction/nonfiction)
- Authors
- Genres
- Other

Then, summarize data by small group or by the whole class:

- Number of books per week
- Types of books (fiction/nonfiction)
- Authors
- Genres
- Other

STUDENT PORTFOLIOS

Best Practice

The student portfolio has been getting a good response from teachers, students, and parents as a feedback tool. A student portfolio is a grand and graphic measure of the growth and development of student learning. It inspires the student to do more and to do it even better than last time. While this data is probably considered soft data compared to the hard data of number of books read, the reading portfolio can be an effective tool for self-assessment, goal setting, and evidence of achieving the goals or movement toward the goals. Helping students maintain and sustain their love of reading and attain the goals they have set for themselves is a mission teachers must embrace.

> **A student portfolio is a grand and graphic measure of the growth and development of student learning.**

Feedback is the food of champion readers.

Teachers can have their students structure their portfolios around the reading from the literature circles or even around biographies from social studies or science. Students can keep "learning lists" of vocabulary words, authors, genres, reflections on particular readings, and so on. The possibilities are limitless, and the feedback is illuminating. After all, feedback is the food of champion readers.

PERFORMANCE LEARNING

Performance learning, in which teachers structure robust projects, authentic performances, and rich learning experiences, lays the groundwork for active hands and engaged minds. When students are involved in inquiry learning, discovery, investigations, and the like, they become intensely invested in the work. The reading becomes part and parcel of the real work they are doing, and they use reading as a tool in their kit. Students become aware of the power of their reading and writing skills as they search and research their topic. A typical performance learning curriculum might include the following:

Problem Based Learning Ideas

Scenarios
> You are a tour guide for Civil War sites. What will you do?

Case Studies
> A Lie Is a Lie! (It's not a lie if you don't tell because it would hurt someone's feelings).

Inventions
> Rube Goldberg Inventions Contest With Simple Machines

Experiments
> Float or Sink? Or How Far Will It Fly?

Investigations
> Crime Scene Investigation: Graffiti in the Schoolyard

Projects
> Adopt a Grandparent: Interviews at the Assisted Living Complex

Themes
> Text Messaging: The Good, The Bad, The Ugly

Mediate With Early Intervention Strategies

---✦---

As discussed earlier, the concept that "the rich get richer and the poor get poorer" is the essence of the research findings called the Matthews Effect (Stanovich, 1986). Over time, good readers read more and more, and poor readers read less and less or not at all. The gap between them in terms of achievement continues to widen. Stop the madness! Intervene in creative and purposeful ways before the gap widens any more.

Teachers must commit to use what they know about the teaching-learning process to help students conquer reading challenges. Intervention in the literacy instruction process does not mean "Teach it louder and slower." It does not mean "Send them to summer school." It does not mean "Keep them back." Intervention means doing things differently and, in this case, doing things differently immediately. It means using explicit strategies to find the entry point for the learner. Intervention means embracing methods for developing reading fluency and enhancing comprehension.

Swift and appropriate interventions are necessary when students are having difficulty with reading. A system of diagnosis and prescription is standard practice; intervention means to note deficiencies in literacy and to address them with appropriate strategies. Intervention is based on the Matthew Effect research in which Stanovich (1986) suggests that the reading gap continues to widen as students progress through school. In other words, even though reading becomes more prevalent in the curriculum as students reach higher grades, readers read more and more while nonreaders read less and less or not at all. In essence, the rich (readers) get richer and the poor (nonreaders) get poorer.

The burning question: How does one intervene successfully? There are many ways to structure reading interventions, as skillful teachers demonstrate all the time. Two particularly powerful interventions are reciprocal teaching (Palincsar & Brown, 1985) and one-to-one tutoring (Bloom, 1981) with Roger Farr's model-coach-reflect (MCR) methodology (Farr, 1999). In addition, the concept of examining student work for cues to improving their skills, through an analysis of their mistakes, is a powerful strategy.

How does one intervene successfully?

Best Practice

RECIPROCAL TEACHING

In this well-researched reading strategy called reciprocal teaching (Palincsar & Brown, 1985), a four-step procedure (summarize, question, clarify, and predict) makes the reading process interactive between the teacher and the text. Initially, the teacher works with small groups of students to model the reciprocal teaching procedures. The teacher reads a paragraph or two and then summarizes what he or she just read. Then, the teacher poses questions for discussion and deliberation. The teacher models how to clarify the meaning of the text and then asks students to make predictions about what might happen next and why.

For example, a teacher asks students to summarize in their own words the information they have just read about the formation of volcanoes. Then, the teacher asks students to generate questions that come to mind as they learn how volcanoes are formed. Once students produce some questions, the teacher makes clarifications and asks students to predict what might occur next in the reading based on their thinking at the moment. As students read to validate the predictions, in essence, they read more intently because the reading has a clear and compelling purpose. The four steps are delineated below.

Reciprocal Teaching Model

Summarize: produce a verbal summary of a reading.

Question: generate questions based on the summary.

Clarify: investigate concerns and revise the summary and the questions for precision and clarity.

Predict: anticipate where the next reading passages will take you, and check your predictions.

In the reciprocal teaching model, after the teacher models the procedure a number of times and explains the process as he or she is modeling it, it is time for students to reciprocate. A designated student leader models the same process the teacher has been demonstrating. The student assumes the role of teacher and repeats the process.

In essence, a student reads a brief portion of text, for example, about the explorers in the New World. The student leader encourages the student reader to summarize in his or her own words what he or she has just read. The student leader proceeds to ask questions about the explorers' adventures. As the student leader clarifies understandings about the reading, he or she elicits predictions by asking other questions: What do you think the explorers are thinking? Feeling? How might you feel in a similar situation? What are their options? What might you do if you were part of this team? In this way, each student, in turn and over time, becomes the student leader and models the read-think strategy of reciprocal teaching.

One by one, students take over responsibility for the active, attentive read-think process of critical readers. The leadership role is reciprocal, turning over responsibility to the students, and, in reciprocating, students eventually internalize the reading process. Reciprocal teaching is a reading strategy that works well as an intervention because it provides a model of reading for students to practice explicitly. It is structured for success as students take on the role of the leader and learn to use the strategies on their own.

The teacher models, and a designated student leader practices by modeling the same process. More specifically, the teacher *summarizes* the reading, poses *questions* that come to mind, *clarifies* concerns, and *predicts* what may happen next in the reading. The process models explicitly what good readers do mentally as they read. As each student takes responsibility for leading the reading discussion, he or she follows the four-step cycle of summarizing, questioning, clarifying, and predicting as readers prepare to move to the next passage in the reading. In this way, students are taught, explicitly, to comprehend fully; they learn how to understand what has been read before they proceed to the next part.

This process demonstrates how readers use the previous information to anticipate the coming information. It shows how good readers make sense of the text as they read, while they read, and after they read. In turn, it prevents poor readers from reading, reading, and reading through the page and coming to the end of the passage or page having no idea what they have just read. It prevents simply word calling, with no comprehension at all, by giving students a specific set of steps to help them understand the text.

Reciprocal teaching prevents simply word calling, with no comprehension at all.

Best Practice

ONE-TO-ONE TUTORING

Another method of intervention is one-to-one tutoring, using the modeling-coaching-reflection (MCR) strategy (Farr, 1999). Teachers can use this strategy before, during, and after reading to help students see how readers comprehend what they are reading.

Before reading, the teacher models the talk-aloud strategy to demonstrate what he or she is thinking about the title of the story. As the teacher thinks aloud about the title, he or she makes predictions about what the reading will be about and gives reasons for those predictions.

At various points during the reading, the teacher stops and thinks aloud, and he or she predicts what will happen next. The teacher talks aloud to explain why he or she is thinking that these things might happen. The teacher uses inferences for implied meaning and talks about how the words suggest certain things.

After the reading, the teacher summarizes his or her interpretation of the text and justifies it with specific examples in the text. The emphasis here is on comprehending what one is reading while one is reading—not on comprehending the reading after the reading. The teacher uses this process—the modeling-coaching-reflection strategy—with that emphasis in mind.

In a one-to-one scenario, the student practices the talk-aloud strategy with appropriate coaching by the teacher. The teacher asks, "Why are you thinking that? What makes you so sure? Where is the evidence in the text?" This coaching leads to a reflective summary by the student of how he or she responded to the reading. The MCR model eventually becomes second nature to students as they learn to read and think while reading.

One-to-one tutoring (Bloom, 1981) is enhanced when teachers couple it with the three procedures outlined by Roger Farr (1999): modeling, coaching, and reflection (MCR). In a one-on-one situation, teachers can explicitly model their behavior while reading aloud, demonstrating the interaction between the text and the thinking of the reader. Then teachers can enter into coached practices with individual learners. During coached practices, teachers provide specific, immediate feedback, which stimulates students to think reflectively. In these coached practices, teachers ask students to say out loud what they are thinking as they read and to give reasons for that thinking.

Coaching in the reading instruction process is a strategy to make the implicit reactions to the reading more explicit. In this way, students can further examine their thought processes as they continue to read. They can examine and reflect on what is occurring in the text and in their minds, and they can anticipate what is about to happen. Teachers mediate this stage for metacognitive reflection with questions that call for student self-monitoring. They ask what connections the student is making, how they might relate the ideas to a personal situation, or, simply, what they think will happen next

According to Bloom (1981), there is no teaching as effective as the one-to-one tutorial.

and why. Often, teachers implement reciprocal teaching with small groups, but when the teacher is able to work with one student, the teacher can choose strategies that are in direct relation to the student's miscues. This creates a diagnosis-prescription cycle tailored to the explicit deficiencies of the reader. It is mediation (Feuerstein, Rand, Hoffman, & Miller, 1980) by the teacher that is direct, intentional, and meaningful. According to Bloom (1981), there is no teaching as effective as the one-to-one tutorial.

EXAMINING STUDENT WORK

Best Practice

Another strategy that helps to mediate the learning with specific interventions is the process of examining student work. By using the results of the analysis to intercede with more appropriate strategies, the teacher gives the student immediate and specific help to target a weakness or area of concern. Typically, the process of examining student work is done collaboratively, with a team of teachers who have similar grade level or department responsibilities.

Various protocols prevail as teachers look over student products and performances. They look for noticeable trends across several samples, as well as for specific patterns for individual students. From the observation and analysis, teams often develop a scoring rubric to delineate the exact elements of the assignment and the range of quality performances from low quality to high. This, in turn, helps teachers and students become more cognizant of the academic expectations. The process clarifies what is wanted and where the strengths and shortfalls occur.

Typical protocols call for a team of teachers, who have similar students, to work together. First, teachers actually perform the assignment themselves. Then, they compare insights, create a listing of concerns that translates into a comprehensive rubric, and examine student samples against the emerging rubric. These protocols are as follows.

Protocols: Examining Student Work

Team of teachers who have similar students formed

Teachers performing the assignment

Comparison of insights

Creation of a comprehensive rubric

Examining student samples with the rubric

ppeal to Parents/Guardians and Get Them Involved

I t takes the combined efforts of the teacher, the student, and the parent/guardian to support the academic schooling of the youngster.

Waxman and Walberg (1999) describe schooling as a three-legged stool. They explain that the first leg of the stool is the teacher, the second leg is the student, and the third leg is the parent/guardian. Without all three legs, the stool is not functional. It takes the combined effort of the three legs to support the stool properly. In other words, it takes the combined efforts of the teacher, the student, and the parent/guardian to support the academic schooling of the youngster.

PARENT INVOLVEMENT

Waxman and Walberg's metaphor embraces research that suggests that parent/guardian involvement in students' school experience is vital. When parents/guardians get involved, student benefits are great. This involvement may mean that parents/guardians volunteer time in the classroom, that they become active in parent groups at the school, or that they simply support the academic efforts of their children at home.

Parent involvement comes in a variety of ways, from helping with homework to volunteering in the classroom or on school committees. See Figure 9.

Parent Involvement

At Home:

Involvement in Homework

Reading to Young Children

Provide Print-rich Environment

At School:

Classroom Volunteer

Field Trip Escort

School Helper

School Committee Member

District Board Member

Figure 9

Of course, the most common involvement at home is parents/guardians helping their children with their homework or at least monitoring the homework situation and seeing that it does get done. By being aware of the assignments and supervising the process, parents/guardians are implicitly supporting their children's academic progress in school. They have some sense of the content students are learning, and they have some connection to the schoolwork.

Another way parents/guardians support the learning of their children, especially in the early grades, is by reading aloud to their children at home or reading along with older children. As one principal tells her parents, "You don't have to read with your child every day, just the days that you eat" (Anonymous respondent at Teaching for Intelligence Conference Literacy Q/A Panel, March 2000, Orlando, FL). She makes her point with humor, but she makes her point. Reading with children is as critical to their growth as food is.

> "You don't have to read with your child every day, just the days that you eat."

This support effort involves creating a home environment that is rich in print materials: magazines, books, booklets, newspapers, and journals. It is also important for students to have library cards and to take frequent trips to borrow books. Students also benefit from seeing their parents/ guardians reading and discussing what they have read. Students see that reading is a lifelong endeavor, and they begin to emulate the parent/ guardian behaviors in literacy.

Getting parents, guardians, the extended family, and even the community at large involved must be a strategic, deliberate, and collaborative goal of classroom teachers and school leaders. Of course, the most common way to do this is through frequent communications and invitations to participate in school activities. Parents/guardians often want to participate in their children's school experience; sometimes they just need some cues about how to do that.

> Parents/guardians often want to participate in their children's school experience; sometimes they just need some cues.

HOMEWORK

Best Practice

Homework is an integral part of the teaching-learning process. It is the time for students to try things on their own—some independent practice. However, involved parents/guardians provide valuable support. They make homework part of the daily routines at home. Simply by scheduling time for homework and providing a place for the student to do the work, parents/guardians send a clear and important message to their children: homework is important.

> Homework is an integral part of the teaching-learning process.

Of course, sometimes students need hands-on help to understand the homework, and many parents willingly get involved at this level when they can or when they understand the process the teacher has outlined. Older siblings can provide some guidance here, too. The important factor is the availability and accessibility of the parent/guardian, family, or extended family in the homework process to provide the necessary support for the student to succeed.

Best practice suggests that educators instruct parents/guardians in how they might best help their children with homework. Teachers can easily delineate the roles parents/guardians play in getting involved in homework matters. For example, parents/guardians can structure a time and a place for homework that becomes a part of their child's routine. Parents/guardians can be available if their child is stuck on an assignment, having their child explain the homework for further clarity and understanding. All of these parent/guardian behaviors send a clear message to the child that the parent/guardian and teacher are partners in schooling. This kind of parent/guardian participation sets a tone of cooperation and collaboration between the school and home.

Best Practice

READ ALOUD

Reading is not just a school activity. Reading is a life skill. Parents/guardians who read at home model the lifelong behavior of reading as a part of everyday life. Parents/guardians who read to their children are giving them the greatest gift of all. They are giving their children the legacy of reading.

Reading is not just a school activity. Reading is a life skill.

Early readers are often those children who have experienced frequent reading at home from the time they were infants. They understand that reading is related to the written word, and they quickly become adept at figuring out letter-sound relationships and acquiring a sight vocabulary.

Teachers can encourage parents/guardians to read to their children in early grades in a number of ways. Teachers can talk to parents/guardians at parent night, send memos home, create a list of instructions to guide the reading aloud at home, or even establish a tracking activity or incentive program to motivate reading at home. Another interesting strategy is to establish a parent-student book club.

The power of reading aloud to young children cannot be overstated. While attending a national conference on reading, an invited panel member told the delegates that they must read to their children—every day. Later, during the question and answer session, an audience member asked, "Do we have to read to our kids every day?" The panelist did not miss a beat, and made her stinging point when she replied, "Oh, no, certainly not every day . . . just on the days that you eat."

"If a young child can recite eight nursery rhymes by the age of four, he or she will be a top reader by the age of eight."

—Mem Fox

Did you know that Mem Fox (Fox & Horacek, 2001) reports that if a young child can recite eight nursery rhymes by the age of four, he or she will be a top reader by the age of eight? Did you know that if parents read one story a day to their child for the first three years of life, that child will have heard 1000 stories by the age of three? Imagine the advantage of these early readers: their extensive vocabulary, sense of story, and richness of background knowledge. These are simple facts with profound repercussions. Pass the word on to parents everywhere. It can make an enormous difference.

"Did you know that if parents read one story a day to their child for the first three years of life, that child will have heard 1000 stories by the age of three?"

—Mem Fox

Teach Vocabulary by Building Background Knowledge

───────────── ✥ ─────────────

The act of reading calls for several critical elements to interact simultaneously: word knowledge, fluency, comprehension, and writing (Cunningham & Hall, 1994; Shanahan, 1998). Students need to develop an extensive vocabulary to read with fluency. In turn, fluency in reading leads to increased comprehension. Fluency also comes from the written language of the reader since the student writes words he or she knows. Increased comprehension enhances the written language of the learner.

> **Students need to develop an extensive vocabulary to read with fluency.**

Students read what they write with fluency and comprehension because it is their story written in their own words—words they know and comprehend. These words comprise the key vocabulary, or the inner language, of learners. These are their "first words," and the "next words" consist of the more formal vocabulary they add to this organic, natural language of their speaking vocabulary.

The concept of adding next words to first words focuses on the element of word knowledge as it relates to reading. Moving from first words to next words is a method of sight vocabulary development that incorporates phonemic awareness, phonics, and structural analyses. Sight words are at the heart of the case for word knowledge as it relates to fluency.

It is important to note that vocabulary development encompasses a speaking/listening vocabulary, as well as a reading/writing vocabulary.

Speaking/listening vocabulary and reading/writing vocabulary are inextricably linked.

While the speaking/listening vocabulary is initially more expansive than the reading/writing vocabulary, both vocabularies are inextricably linked in the mind of the learner. In fact, the speaking/listening vocabulary often provides the cues for the rhythm and sound of the language that translates into the reading/writing vocabulary. And, at the same time, the reading/writing vocabulary can enrich and enhance the speaking/listening vocabulary through a richness of topics that the reader may encounter or write spontaneously.

Teachers can strengthen this link in powerful ways with organic reading and writing programs (Ashton-Warner, 1972) that tap into the natural language of the learner. In this type of program, the inner language of the learner is used to provide a personal vocabulary. The student uses these first words to build written stories that encourage fluent reading. Sylvia Ashton-Warner devised this method of teaching reading to Maori children in New Zealand to facilitate learning for 5- to 12-year-olds who spoke only their native language. In trying to teach the children to read English, she began with the organic vocabulary, which she called the key vocabulary, or words in their native tongue—words from their inner selves. She wrote stories with this vocabulary for the children to read, and the children wrote their own stories to read. Gradually, she transitioned the children into proper English.

In essence, organic reading and writing programs suggest ways for students to write words from their speaking/listening vocabulary and to use organic word collections to spark the reading and writing processes. Students can manipulate a personally relevant listing of words into written pieces that they can read with fluency and understanding. Students can collect their words over time on word cards, which they can place in word boxes (Showers et al., 1998) or in vocabulary logs or journals. Students manage the boxes, logs, or journals as the owner of the words and update them on a regular basis. Students routinely keep the individual lists current, which encourages meaningful use in reading and writing activities. Accompanied with a more structured and formal reading program, the development of an organic vocabulary for the reading, writing, speaking, and listening processes facilitates the overall literacy skills of the learner.

ABC GRAFFITI

Best Practice

A marvelous and engaging strategy to generate vocabulary is called ABC Graffiti. In this activity, students work in pairs. Focusing on the target word, they begin by writing the alphabet down the left-hand side of the page. Then, they use the alphabet as an advance organizer and brainstorm a word for each letter of the alphabet that describes or relates to the target word. For example, if the target word were *war*, the list might read *aggression, battle, conflict, destruction*, and so on. While they do not have to go in any order, the abc pattern becomes quite a compelling motivator. Students rarely stop until they have each and every letter filled in. The activity allows students to unpack the meaning of the target word and, at the same time, to produce a rich list of words. This is a perfect activity for concepts in various subject areas:

A marvelous and engaging strategy to generate vocabulary is called ABC Graffiti.

Math: symmetry, fractions, probability

Science: cycle, hypothesis, experiment

Social Science: democracy, power, war

Language Arts: genre, protagonist, essay

Arts: melody, perspective, drama

Health/Physical Education: cardiovascular, fitness, exercise

WORD COLLECTIONS

Best Practice

Word Boxes

Building a fluent vocabulary through the use of personal word boxes is an easy strategy to use across the disciplines. This is how readers use their natural language and speaking vocabulary to develop a personal reading vocabulary or key vocabulary, as Sylvia Ashton-Warner called it. It is also an effective method for students to build vocabulary in core content areas.

In the early grades, students can decorate shoeboxes to create personal word boxes. To help students gather new words each day, the teacher keeps a supply of 8-inch by 3-inch colored construction paper strips in a coffee can. As students go to the teacher to select their special or key word for the day, they ask the teacher to print the word on the strip. They then trace it, say it, and use it in context before leaving the teacher.

As students collect words on word cards, they use the words in their own boxes to play "Go Fish" with a partner. They usually play the card game as soon as they come into the room. They dump the cards from both boxes on the floor and then "Go Fish" for their word cards. Students mix their cards with a partner. Then each student takes a turn picking up a word that is facedown and tries to say the word. If the student knows the word, he or she keeps it and puts it in the word box. If the student does not know the word, he or she puts it back in the pile. If there are any leftover words that no one claims, they are simply thrown away. That way, the owner of the box knows all words in the box and can use them easily in writing and other work.

After students play "Go Fish" with their old words, they are ready for a new word. They then go to the teacher for the word they want for that day. Students may have any word they want. They usually select a word that means something to them. The word is part of some experience or instance in their lives.

The teacher may then have students study their words by using paints, sand, shells, clay, water, blocks, computers, pantomime or song to create the letters and spell the words. Once students study their new words, have students put their word strips together to create a story. Stories can be a few words, a phrase, or a sentence or two. Provide function words (the, and, is, this) as needed on neutral color strips.

Make sure students write their sentences each day. In the beginning, the "sentence" may consist of only one word, usually a noun. As students add verbs, the sentences eventually grow in length and complexity. Encourage students to add a cover and pictures to illustrate their stories. Change the word strip color each month so the covers of the storybooks and word strips are the same color. In this way, students create storybooks each month with a colorful cover that matches the words in the word boxes for the month. Much like student portfolios, these storybooks show the developmental progress of the learner. September's booklets and stories look different when compared to January's, as January's storybooks look different when compared to June's.

Send the storybooks featuring these "organic word stories" home, and ask students to read their books to everyone and then gather signatures for a weekly classroom contest. Encourage students to read their storybooks to Mom, Dad, other family members, friends, or neighbors. Each time students read their booklets, have them gather signatures from "witnesses." The goal is to get them to read the books many times and to read with fluency and comprehension. In essence, students learn to read fluently as this speaking vocabulary becomes their reading and writing vocabulary.

> Students learn to read fluently as this speaking vocabulary becomes their reading and writing vocabulary.

Journals and Logs

To develop vocabulary for the older students, word logs or vocabulary journals serve the same purpose as the word boxes. Again, students can use these growing lists of words in their writing or to better understand content-specific reading material. Vocabulary journals or logs work on the same principle as the word boxes, but are geared for the older, more mature students.

Vocabulary Logs

Use vocabulary logs to build vocabulary around the content of disciplines through analysis skills, root words, and derivatives. Have science words, social studies words, and a literature vocabulary to facilitate learning words by themes. Help students become aware and eventually skillful in using word analysis to figure out unknown words.

Little Books

Little books are paper foldables that provide a place and a purpose for writing, summarizing, and synthesizing information. Directions for the little book appear in Figure 10 below.

Little books are paper foldables that provide a place and a purpose for writing, summarizing, and synthesizing information.

Directions: The Little Book

1. Fold a sheet of paper in half the short way (a hamburger bun or a taco fold). Then fold it in half again, into four corners; and fold it in half one more time. When you open the paper, it will have eight sections.

2. Now, fold the paper again into the hamburger bun. Keep the fold at the top and tear along the center vertical through the fold to the horizontal mark, half way down. If you did this correctly, there should be a hole in the middle of the paper that you can look through.

3. After the tear has been made, refold the paper the long way, like a hot dog bun or a burrito. The fold and the hole are on the top.

4. Hold both ends of the hotdog fold and push the ends toward the center—(your hands are pushing toward each other)—until all four sections touch. It looks kind of like a pinwheel.

5. Then, gently fold the pages around, and you have a little book with a cover and seven pages.

6. Put the ragged edges on the bottom, and you are ready to write on the cover.

Figure 10

Rings

Simple metal rings can be used to collect a personal set of words. Students use word cards and add cards to the ring for quick reference. The ring of words can target one subject area, a story or unit, or general word gathering all day long.

Word Walls

Well known and popular, word walls are seen often in classrooms, as students are surrounded by the key words of their school day.

Best Practice

FOUR-FOLD CONCEPT DEVELOPMENT

The four-fold activity is a strategy to build vocabulary and develop a concept. It can be used with an individual student, pairs, or a small group of students. The paper (regular copy paper or large poster paper, depending on the number of students) is folded in four sections as indicated in Figure 11. When the paper is folded, the corners where the folds meet is turned down to create a triangle; once it is opened, there will be a diamond shape in the center of the paper for the target word. Each of the four sections is labeled from left to right starting at the top left and ending at the bottom right: LIST, RANK, COMPARE, ILLUSTRATE.

Then each section is addressed as the students unpack the language of the target word.

In the example, the target word is from language arts. It is the noun "plot," meaning the plot of a story. Students follow these four steps:

1. LIST: Brainstorm 15–20 synonyms.

2. RANK: Prioritize the top three words, the best words to clarify the word "plot."

3. COMPARE: Students use the following to create an analogy:

   "Target Word" is like (Concrete/tangible word) because both

   1.

   2.

   3.

4. ILLUSTRATE: Draw a visual metaphor of the analogy; make a poster.

Four-Fold Concept Development	
LIST plan scheme story line action drama play	*RANK* Scheme Story Line Action
COMPARE "Plot" is like map because both 1. Lay out the plan 2. Develop a route to follow 3. Give or create a picture	*ILLUSTRATE* 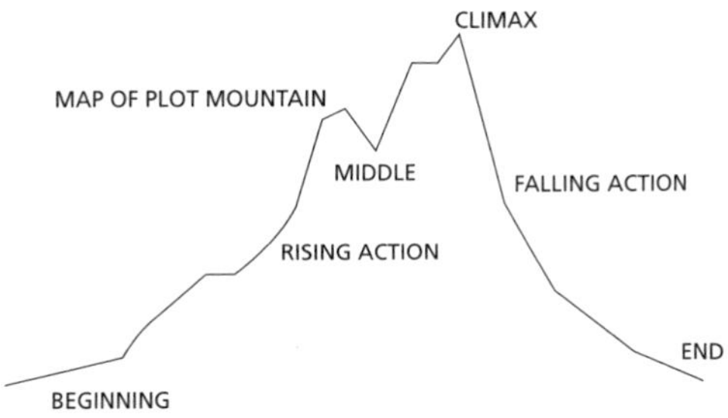

Figure 11

Once the four steps are completed, students can share the information. The process helps develop vocabulary and concepts and can be used with target words from any subject area. Possible words to use that are key concepts in the various disciplines might include

Math: distributive, associative, infinity, equal, algebra

Language Arts: comprehension, literature, fiction, nonfiction

Science: energy, motion, environment, chemistry, physics

Social Sciences: Bill of Rights, Civil War, citizenship, election

Health/Physical Education: wellness, sportsmanship, genes, muscles, nutrition

Arts: media, medium, sculpture, comedy, tragedy, opera

Tune In to Technology to Impact Literacy

———— ✥ ————

Technology impacts reading in positive ways. As anyone who has a computer nearby knows, the compulsion to go to the computer is always there. It beckons one to write, to compute, to create graphics, to preview films, to purchase online books, to download news articles, to e-mail a friend, to surf the World Wide Web, or just to check the weather. It calls one to use all the skills of literacy: reading, writing, speaking, and listening. Once one answers the call, it is very hard to shut that computer down and move on to other tasks. The computer has a compelling quality not unlike a magnet. Once one logs onto the computer, the pull to stay is great—no matter what the age of the user.

Technology impacts reading in positive ways.

The computer just might be the motivation students need to get hooked on literacy.

Because of this inherent attraction to technology, teachers would do well not to overlook the power of this enticing tool. The computer just might be the motivation students need to get hooked on literacy ("Technology counts," 1998, 1999). When students work in pairs or small groups to coach and support each other as they explore technological innovations, their engagement in literacy becomes seamless. Think about the possibility for the "i-generation"—the information generation.

Literacy online is what it is all about. Literacy online is the format for the new millennium: word processing for letters, stories, and essays; e-mail to communicate with classmates, friends, parents/guardians, and pen pals around the world; spreadsheets to organize and analyze data and feedback; graphic design programs for school and class presentations; and the Internet for research. The possibilities are endless as students in today's schools gain more access to computers and as the power of technology becomes fully realized as a champion for the literacy challenge.

LITERACY ONLINE

Literacy online is a way to make technology a part of literacy and learning. Students can use the computer for word processing, e-mail, spreadsheets, graphical presentations, and research to stimulate reading and writing processes. Teachers can use peer editors and partner work and teach Internet formats and strategies (formatting for e-mail and chat rooms, what and when to download, what and when to just read online, and so on).

Technology is an entry point for motivating literacy skills.

Literacy online has its own form and function protocols that teachers need to include in the curriculum. Use the following formats purposefully and frequently in classroom activities:

E-mail

- Communicating with other classrooms, schools, parents/guardians, pen pals
- Contacting experts in a particular field under study

Research

- Searching the Internet to research a topic and to learn how to search, survey, prioritize, and critically evaluate
- Using information efficiently and intelligently for purposeful learning

Text Messaging

- Using text messaging shorthand to communicate via wireless networks with cell phones and similar technology advances

Web-based Online Programs

- Accessing programs such as Skills Tutor or Accelerated Reader as motivational tools for reading interventions

Blogs

- Creating student-authored blogs or daily or weekly interactive columns that are authored by students purporting points of views on various political or civic topics of interest

WORD/NUMERACY PROCESSING

Best Practice

Word Processing

- Writing, editing (using cut-and-paste functions, checking spelling and grammar, and learning about find-and-replace functions to search for and correct common errors), rewriting, formatting (using fonts and bold or italic type), keyboarding
- Comparing and contrasting rambling text that has poor spelling and grammar errors to clear, concise, orderly text written with purpose and direction

Spreadsheets

- Collecting, organizing, and manipulating data
- Developing budgets or recording other numerical data

GRAPHIC ARTS

Best Practice

Slide Presentations

- Adding graphics, slides, and sound to presentations, speeches, book reports, or even show-and-tell

Illustrations

- Creating illustrations and art for stories, poems, dramas, or essays

Enter Literacy With a Multiple Intelligences Approach

Howard Gardner's (1983) work in the area of multiple intelligences has produced a theory that is embraced fully by the educational community. Basically, the theory states that the human mind has multiple intelligences, as opposed to the notion of general intelligence traditionally held. Using a number of criteria, Gardner has identified eight intelligences to date: verbal/linguistic, visual/spatial, mathematical/logical, musical/rhythmic, bodily/kinesthetic, interpersonal/social, intrapersonal/reflective, and the naturalist/physical world.

Gardner postulates a possible ninth intelligence or, as he has called it, the eight-and-one-half intelligence—the existential or cosmic intelligence. He is looking to neurologists for information on a processing locale in the brain for the big questions about life and the universe—the philosophical questions that are pondered by poets and priests and people of all ages and in all stages of life.

Gardner defines an intelligence as a way of creating products or solving problems that are valued in at least one culture. He suggests that there are many ways of knowing and of expressing what one knows about the world and that schooling might use all entry points for learners. These entry points tap into the strengths of the

> **Gardner defines an intelligence as a way of creating products or solving problems that are valued in at least one culture.**

individual learners and allow them entry into the learning. The skillful teacher uses a repertoire of strategies based on the eight intelligences.

The intelligences are defined briefly below with some examples to illustrate their various manifestations in K–12 classrooms.

Verbal/Linguistic

Reading, writing, speaking, listening (e.g., drama, stories, narratives, expository writing, speeches, debates, dialogues)

Visual/Spatial

Art, graphics, architecture, sculpture, mapping, navigation (e.g., perspectives, images, advertising, billboards, the imaginary world)

Mathematical/Logical

Mathematics, science, logic, deductive thinking, inductive reasoning (e.g., geometry, algebra, calculus, formulas and equations, categorizing, ranking, outlining, argumentation)

Musical/Rhythmic

Music, rhythm and beat (e.g., composing, singing, playing an instrument, band, orchestra, quartets, symphonies, harmonies, poetry, choral recitation, clapping responses)

Bodily/Kinesthetic

Hands-on activities, manipulatives (e.g., lab work, field trips and experiential learning, role-plays, drama, acting)

Interpersonal/Social

Cooperating, collaborating (e.g., teamwork, leadership, communicating, resolving conflicts, mediating, building relationships)

Intrapersonal/Reflective

Inner self, metacognition (e.g., self-awareness, self-regulatory, self-monitoring, self-assessing, awareness of strengths and weaknesses)

Naturalist/Physical World

Nature and environmental understandings, classifications (e.g., awareness of flora and fauna, classification of species, nature walks and expeditions)

The theory of multiple intelligences provides a viable framework for academic understandings. As teachers tap these various intelligences, they provide students with numerous entry points into literacy and learning. Students can read music; they can read faces; they can read charts, graphs, and illustrations; and they can read words. Students can read directions, instructions, factual data, and fine literature. As a result, when students face a complex task, they can engage several intelligences to unravel the intricate layers of thinking and performing to complete the task.

MULTIPLE INTELLIGENCES PROFILE

Best Practice

To develop awareness of the multiple intelligences, organize eight different activities that cause students to use the various intelligences specifically. For example, a teacher may use some optical illusions for students to measure their abilities in the visual/ spatial intelligence. As students complete the activities, have them create a personal bar graph of their own personal profiles. Before students begin the activities, have them fold an 8-inch by 11-inch piece of paper into eight vertical folds—similar to a paper fan. Have them label each bar (created by the folds) as an intelligence. The chart serves as a bar graph of sorts, as students mark each bar low, medium, or high based on their personal evaluation of each of their intelligences.

As the graph builds, encourage students to share their profiles with others. Typically, they begin to see why it is beneficial to have very different profiles on a team because they complement each other. In this way, students can celebrate the diversity in a team and become aware of the strengths and weaknesses in the various intelligences, especially in the verbal/linguistic, the logical/mathematical and the visual/spatial areas, which impact most directly on literacy skills.

> **Students can celebrate the diversity in a team and become aware of the strengths and weaknesses in the various intelligences.**

MULTIPLE INTELLIGENCES GRID

Best Practice

To have students become involved in developing literacy activities for each of the eight intelligences, use the planning tool called the MI Grid (see Figure 12).

The Multiple Intelligences (MI) Grid

Verbal/Linguistic	Logical/ Mathematical	Visual/Spatial	Bodily/ Kinesthetic

Musical/ Rhythmic	Interpersonal/ Social	Intrapersonal/ Reflective	Naturalist/ Physical Work

Figure 12

Using the headings for the eight intelligences (visual, verbal, musical, mathematical, bodily, interpersonal, intrapersonal, naturalist), have a team of students work together to brainstorm lists of literacy activities and learning experiences for each intelligence. Then, using the MI Grid of activities to tap into all the intelligences, have students select from the various activities as they take ownership for their own learning. Teachers may want to require one activity choice for each of the intelligences to give some balance to the types of activities students do.

SUSTAINED SILENT READING

Best Practice

The concept of sustained silent reading (SSR) is revisited by Marzano (2004) in *Building Background Knowledge* as one of the two most powerful strategies to develop vocabulary for increased fluency and comprehension in reading. SSR is based on the premise that the student selects a book of high interest and appropriate reading level. Using a multiple intelligences approach to SSR fosters self-selection and self-assessment for students as they learn to accommodate their strengths and weaknesses in learning. In this model, it is recommended that students find a book of choice and read silently and continuously for 20–30 minutes, at least three times a week.

Read Aloud, Read Along, Read Appropriately to Foster Flexible Readers

Based on the framework of the National Assessment of Educational Progress (NAEP, 1998), there are three types of reading that dictate student proficiency: narratives (for literary experiences), informational reading (for facts, data, and a knowledge base), and procedural reading (for following directions and understanding technical works).

Further suggested in this model are four levels of reading: initial understanding, interpretation, developing a personal response, and evaluating. To help students become efficient and flexible readers moving through the different levels of proficiency, the three strategies of read aloud, read along, and read appropriately play different roles.

Reading aloud gives students the opportunity to hear the sound and rhythm of the language. As the teacher thinks aloud about what he or she is reading, the students begin to understand the connections between the words on the page and what they mean. When students read orally, they, too, can hear the words as they process them.

Reading aloud gives students the opportunity to hear the sound and rhythm of the language.

In the read along strategy, teachers provide needed word prompts and cues, as well as fluency in the reading act. As students follow along, their pacing is propelled by the fluency of the reader. The read along activity is a reading exercise for the classroom and for the home. Parents/guardians and older siblings can read orally as the student reads along.

Surprisingly, the fluent reader can read along at quite a brisk pace, and the student somehow seems to keep up, carried along by the flow of the oral reading. (When read-alongs are employed as a strategy for fluency, do not point to the words, but rather place a paper marker beneath the line being read).

The read appropriately strategy promotes the policy of reading material at an appropriate instructional level for greatest individual gains. The adage "different strokes for different folks" applies well here. Because readers respond differently to the reading and writing process, their skill level is critical to their developmental progress. Read aloud, read along, and read appropriately are a triad of strategies that effectively achieve the results teachers want.

Discuss the NAEP framework for types of reading and levels of comprehension to inform students of the various types of reading. In this way, teachers expose learners to the idea of flexible reading for different purposes. Included in the types of reading are narratives for literary experiences, informative texts for information gathering, and procedural steps for following directions. Demonstrate each type. Then discuss or think about the levels of reading comprehension: initial understanding, interpretation, personal response, evaluation. Develop a rubric with students that helps them begin to assess their own levels of understanding about their reading (see Figure 13). Discuss the differences and make them aware of the ultimate goal—achieving a deep understanding of the reading.

Read aloud, read along, and read appropriately strategies involve three phases of reading instruction.

Best Practice

READ ALOUD

Story Time: Using juvenile literature books to highlight the idea of being literate is a powerful strategy for youngsters to use as they read to younger students. Several of the best books include *Leo the Late Bloomer* by Robert Kraus, *Thank You, Mr. Falker* by Patricia Polacco, and *The Jolly Postman* by Janet and Allan Ahlberg.

Readers' Theater: This read aloud approach calls on a group of students to take on roles to read, as they perform a dramatic reading. It creates a natural flow to reading aloud, set apart from the usual round robin reading. In this case, students read when their roles appear in the text. It seems to be highly motivating and engaging to students of various ages.

Rubric				
	INITIAL	**INTERPRETIVE**	**PERSONAL**	**EVALUATIVE**
NARRATIVE	Retells	Makes sense of text	Relates to	Critiques
INFORMATIVE	Summarizes	Makes connections	Uses analogy	Reads critically
PROCEDURAL	Repeats	Rephrases	Adapts	Edits essence

Figure 13

READ ALONG

Echo Reading: When students read side by side and echo read, they basically read in tandem. This affords students the advantage of seeing, saying, and hearing the words and the sound of the language as they read.

Partner Reading: By alternating paragraphs, sections, or pages, students have a companion reader to spark their read-alongs.

READ APPROPRIATELY

The Rule of Five: When students count (on their fingers) five unknown words from one page, the book is probably too difficult. It is called "the rule of five," but it is a simple, folksy assessment for finding an appropriate level book.

Strategize With Guided Reading Activities

"Reading is reading is reading" is not the whole story. Reading takes on many forms. Reading is glancing through a piece, skimming and scanning for key thoughts or ideas. Reading is singing the lyrics from a page of music to the melodic accompaniment of a piano. Reading is scrutinizing an essay for needed edits, revisions, and rewrites. Reading is done in many ways for many reasons, and it involves many contexts, skills, interactions, and metacognitive tasks.

Use a four-corner framework to delineate the classroom climate, the skills needed, interaction patterns, and metacognitive reflection. Use the four-corner framework to tie literacy to the microcosm of the classroom (see Figure 14). When you set a climate, create a safe emotional space for learning to read. Foster a safe environment in which students have choices about their reading. Also, make sure that students have challenging books to read within a print-rich environment that offers rigor and robustness in reading materials.

When you teach skills, provide direct instruction of reading skills including phonemic awareness to emphasize sounds; phonics for sound word relationships; and configurational, contextual, and structural clues to enhance vocabulary and fluency.

When you structure student interaction, consider meaningful learning experiences, including literature circles (Bjorklund et al., 1998),

The Four-Corner Framework

Setting the Climate *for* Thinking	Teaching the Skills *of* Thinking
Emotions Choice Challenge Print Rich	Phonemic Awareness Phonics Configural Clues Contextual Clues
Structuring the Interaction *With* Thinking	Thinking *About* Thinking
Literature Circles Peer Editing Readers' Theater Preferences	Reflections Reading Response Journals Data and Feedback Read Aloud

Figure 14

in which small groups share the reading and discussion of a story or novel, or incorporate peer mediation or editing, readers' theater, drama, and read aloud opportunities.

Finally, when you encourage metacognition, or thinking about thinking, provide opportunities for written and oral reflections, reading response journals in which students respond to the reading by writing a journal entry, data and feedback loops, and opportunities for students to think about their reading preferences.

Always remember that, as the purpose for reading changes, the way one reads changes with it. Look at two very different kinds of reading: reading a short story or reading a textbook. Reading a short story is invitational, as the plot line heightens and the reader anticipates what will happen next. The purpose of reading a short story is often entertainment.

Reading a textbook is quite different. It is reading for information to gain an understanding and a knowledge base about the topic at hand.

For some, it is a tedious kind of reading, requiring an especially attentive mind to absorb the essential information.

In both these cases, one can apply different strategies to guide the reading. In fact, two popular guided reading strategies that are effective and direct interventions are the Directed Reading and Thinking Activity (DRTA) (Stauffer, 1969) and the Survey, Question, Read, Recite, and Review (SQ3R) method (Robinson, 1970).

The DRTA strategy lends itself to the short story or other fictional pieces as it directs the reader to use the think ahead, read, and think back strategy as he or she proceeds through the piece. On the other hand, the SQ3R is perfectly tailored for textbook reading. Survey the chapter for boldface type, graphics, and questions at the end; form key questions to answer while reading; read; recite answers; and review as needed.

DIRECTED READING AND THINKING ACTIVITY (DRTA)

Best Practice

To use the strategic reading strategy called the DRTA, select a fictional piece for reading and chart out appropriate sections of the story by drawing a line beneath each section to separate it from the next part. Have students make predictions about the story by telling partners what they think will happen in that section. Be sure to have them justify their predictions. Then have them read to validate their predictions. Get them to infer, or read between the lines, about a character's feelings and the mood of the story or setting by trying to go beyond the given information. Continue directing the reading by sections with predictions, justifications, inferences, and validations. Direct the reading and the thinking activity, and see what happens with students' reading comprehension.

BET STRATEGY

Best Practice

The use of the thinking skill called prediction primes the pump and gets students to tap into prior knowledge and background experiences. The BET strategy works really well to get students to predict. BET stands for the following:

Base on fact

Express possibilities

Tender your bet

> Prediction primes the pump and gets students to tap into prior knowledge.

Teachers can chunk the reading and have students use the BET cycle. Begin with the title of the piece. Ask students in small groups to look at the facts presented in the title, to think of the possibilities of what the story is about, and then to choose one possibility of what will happen in the story (their bet). Write the bet on large poster paper. Share some of the students' predictions with the whole group. Then have students read in their groups to validate their bets. Students are now reading with a purpose—to see if they are right or wrong.

Continue through a short piece until students understand the BET strategy. At another time, have them try the same strategy with a nonfiction piece from a textbook. Let them discuss how the BET strategy helps them think and read at the same time.

SURVEY, QUESTION, READ, RECITE, AND REVIEW (SQ3R)

To use the SQ3R strategy for reading a nonfiction piece, walk through the SQ3R method with the students using a chapter from a textbook.

Survey the chapter (headings, subheadings, illustrations, charts, graphics, questions within and at the end of the chapter)

Question (i.e., formulate questions to answer as a check on the main ideas and important information in the chapter)

Read by sections

Recite in your own words what you just read

Review to validate your thinking

Once students have tried the SQ3R method as a guided activity, discuss their reactions to it and the pros and cons. Then have them try the same process in small groups, assigning roles and responsibilities for the questioning, reading, reciting, and reviewing.

Encourage students to use the SQ3R strategy on their own and give some feedback on it.

Bibliography

Allington, R. (1983). The reading instruction provided readers of differing abilities. *Elementary School Journal, 83,* 548–559.

Anderson, R., Hiebert, C., Scott, J. A., & Wilkinson, I. (1985). *Becoming a nation of readers.* Champaign: University of Illinois, Center for the Study of Reading.

Armstrong, T. (2003). *The multiple intelligences of reading and writing.* Alexandria, VA: Association for Supervision and Curriculum Development.

Ashton-Warner, S. (1972). *Teacher.* New York: Vinton.

Berliner, D., & Casanova, U. (1993). *Putting research to work.* Arlington Heights, IL: SkyLight Training and Publishing.

Bjorklund, B., Handler, N., Mitten, J., & Stockwell, G. (1998). *Literature circles: A tool for developing students as critical readers, writers, and thinkers.* Paper presented at the 47th annual conference of the Connecticut Reading Association, Waterbury, CT.

Block, C., & Israel, S. (2005). *Reading first and beyond.* Thousand Oaks, CA: Corwin Press.

Bloom, B. (1981). *All our children learning: A primer for parents, teachers, and educators.* New York: McGraw-Hill.

Burns, B. (2006). *How to teach balanced reading and writing* (3rd ed.). Thousand Oaks, CA: Corwin Press.

Cawalti, G. (1995). *Handbook of research on improving student achievement.* Arlington, VA: Educational Research Service.

Chall, J. (1983). *Learning to read: The great debate.* New York: McGraw-Hill.

Coles, G. (2004). Danger in the classroom: 'Brain glitch' research and learning to read. *Phi Delta Kappan, 85*(5), 344–351.

Cunningham, P. (n.d.). *Practical phonics activities that build skills and teach strategies.* Torrence, CA: Staff Development Resources.

Cunningham, P., & Hall, D. (1994). *Making words: Multi-level, hands-on developmentally appropriate spelling and phonics activities.* Torrence, CA: Good Apple.

Diamond, M., & Hopson, J. (1998). *Magic trees of the mind: How to nurture your child's intelligence, creativity and healthy emotions from birth through adolescence.* New York: Dutton.

English, E. W. (1999). *Gift of literacy for the multiple intelligences classroom.* Thousand Oaks, CA: Corwin Press.

Farr, R. (1999). Putting it together: Solving the reading assessment puzzle. In S. J. Barrentine (Ed.), *Reading assessment: Principles and practices for elementary teachers* (pp. 44–56). Newark, DE: International Reading Association.

Feuerstein, R., Rand, Y., Hoffman, M. B., & Miller, R. (1980). *Instrumental enrichment.* Baltimore: University Park Press.

Flavell, J. (1979). Metacognition and cognitive monitoring: A new area of cognitive-development inquiry. *American Psychologist, 34,* 906–911.

Fogarty, R. (1994). *The mindful school: How to teach for metacognitive reflection.* Arlington Heights, IL: IRI/SkyLight Training and Publishing.

Fogarty, R. (2001a). *Differentiated learning: Different strokes for different folks.* Chicago, IL: Robin Fogarty & Associates.

Fogarty, R. (2001b). *Ten things new teachers need to succeed.* Thousand Oaks, CA: Corwin Press.

Fogarty, R. (2002). *Brain-compatible classroom.* Thousand Oaks, CA: Corwin Press.

Fogarty, R., & Pete, B. (2005a). *Close the achievement gap.* Chicago, IL: Robin Fogarty & Associates.

Fogarty, R., & Pete, B. (2005b). *How to differentiate: Curriculum, instruction, and assessment.* Chicago, IL: Robin Fogarty & Associates.

Fox, M., & Horacek, J. (2001). *Reading magic: Why reading aloud to our children will change their lives forever.* Fort Washington, PA: Harvest Books.

Fox, M., & Vivas, J. (1989). *Wilfred Gordon McDonald Partridge.* LaJolla, CA: Kane/Miller Book Publishers.

Gardner, H. (1983). *Frames of mind: The theory of multiple intelligences.* New York: Basic Books.

Gregory, V., & Nikas, J. (2004). *The learning communities guide to improving reading instruction.* Thousand Oaks, CA: Corwin Press.

Gutin, J. (1996). A brain that talks. *Discover, 17*(6), 83–90.

Johnson, D., Johnson, R., Holubec, E. J., & Roy, P. (1984). *Circles of learning: Cooperation in the classroom.* Alexandria, VA: Association for Supervision and Curriculum Development.

Joyce, B. R. (1999a). Reading about reading. *The Reading Teacher, 52*(7), 662–671.

Joyce, B. R. (1999b). The great literacy problem and success for all. *Phi Delta Kappan, 81*(2), 129–133.

Joyce, B. R., & Wolf, J. (1996). Readersville: Building a culture of readers and writers. In B. Joyce & E. Calhoun (Eds.), *Learning experiences in school renewal* (pp. 95–96). Eugene, OR: ERIC Clearinghouse.

Keene, E. O., & Zimmerman, S. (1997). *Mosaic of thought: Teaching comprehension in a reader's workshop.* Portsmouth, NH: Heinemann.

Kesselman-Turkle, J., & Peterson, F. (1981). *Test-taking strategies.* Chicago: Contemporary Books.

Marzano, R. (2004). *Building background knowledge for academic achievement: Research on what works in schools.* Alexandria, VA: Association for Supervision and Curriculum Development.

Miller, L. L. (1980). *Developing reading efficiency.* Minneapolis, MN: Burgess Publishing Company.

National Assessment of Educational Progress (NAEP). (1998). Long term trends in student reading performance. *NAEP Facts, 3*(1).

Ogle, D. (1989). Implementing strategic teaching. *Educational Leadership, 46*(4), 47–48, 57–60.

Palincsar, A. S., & Brown, A. L. (1985). Reciprocal teaching: Activities to promote reading with your mind. In T. L. Harris & E. J. Cogen (Eds.), *Reading, thinking and concept development: Strategies for the classroom* (pp. 147–158). New York: College Board.

Palocco, P. (1998). *Thank you, Mr. Falker.* New York: Philomel Books.

Pearson, P. D. (1986). Twenty years of research in comprehension. In T. E. Raphael (Ed.), *The context of school-based literacy* (pp. 43–62). New York: Random House.

Pete, B., & Fogarty, R. (2003a). *Nine best practices that make the difference.* Chicago, IL: Robin Fogarty & Associates.

Pete, B., & Fogarty, R. (2003b). *Twelve brain principles that make the difference.* Chicago, IL: Robin Fogarty & Associates.

Robinson, F. P. (1970). *Effective study.* New York: Harper & Row.

Rothstein, E., & Lauber, G. (2000). *Writing as learning: A content-based approach* (2nd ed.). Thousand Oaks, CA: Corwin Press.

Shanahan, T. (1998). Twelve studies that have influenced K–12 reading instruction. *Illinois Reading Council Journal, 26*(1), 50–58.

Showers, B., Joyce, B., Scalon, M., & Schnaubelt, C. (1998). A second chance to learn to read. *Educational Leadership, 55*(6), 27–31.

Silverstein, S. (1974). *Where the sidewalk ends: Poems & drawings.* New York: HarperCollins.

Slavin, R. E. (1983). *Cooperative learning.* New York: Longman.

Sollman, C., Emmons, B., & Paolini, J. (1994). *Through the cracks.* New York: Sterling.

Sousa, D. (2004). *How the brain learns to read.* Thousands Oaks, CA: Corwin Press.

Stahl, S. A. (1992). Saying the "p" word: Nine guidelines for exemplary phonics instruction. *The Reading Teacher, 46*(1), 38–44.

Stanovich, K. E. (1986). Matthew effects in reading: Same consequences of individual differences in the acquisition of literacy. *Reading Research Quarterly, 21*(4), 360–406.

Starrett, E. V. (2000). *The mindful school: Teaching phonics for balanced reading.* Arlington Heights, IL: SkyLight Training and Publishing.

Stauffer, R. (1969). *Teaching reading as a thinking process.* New York: Harper and Row.

Sylwester, R. (1995). *A celebration of neurons: An educator's guide to the human brain.* Alexandria, VA: Association for Supervision and Curriculum Development.

Sylwester, R. (Ed.). (1999). *Student brains, school issues: A collection of articles.* Thousand Oaks, CA: Corwin Press.

Technology counts `98: Putting school technology to the test [Special issue]. (1998, October 1). *Education Week.*

Technology counts `99: Building the digital curriculum [Special issue]. (1999, September 23). *Education Week.*

Tovani, C. (2000). *I read it but I don't get it: Comprehension strategies for adolescent readers.* Portland, ME: Stenhouse Publishers.

United States Department of Education. (1986). *What works: Research about teaching and learning.* Washington, DC: Author.

Waxman, H. C., & Walberg, H. J. (Eds.). (1999). *New directions for teaching practice and research*. Berkeley, CA: McCutchan Publishing.

Wayman, J. (1980). *The Other Side of Reading*. Carthage, IL: Good Apple Press.

Wingert, P., & Kantrowitz, B. (1997, October 27). Why Andy couldn't read. *Newsweek, 130*, 57–60, 62–64.

Wisconsin Department of Education. *Strategic learning in the content areas*. Madison, WI: Author.

Wolfe, P., & Nevills, P. (2004). *Building the reading brain, PreK–3*. Thousand Oaks, CA: Corwin Press.

Index

CORWIN PRESS

The Corwin Press logo—a raven striding across an open book—represents the union of courage and learning. Corwin Press is committed to improving education for all learners by publishing books and other professional development resources for those serving the field of PreK–12 education. By providing practical, hands-on materials, Corwin Press continues to carry out the promise of its motto: **"Helping Educators Do Their Work Better."**